HONG KONG dos & don'ts

in HONG KONG

By
Mary Leong / Colin Storey

Illustrations by
Mark Liu Chi Wai

ISBN 1-84464-005-1

Copyright © 2005 Book Promotion and Service Co., Ltd.

Published in Thailand by
Book Promotion and Service Co., Ltd.
2220/31 Ramkhamhaeng 36/1
Huamark, Bangkok 10240
Thailand
Tel: +66 2 7320243-5
Fax: +66 2 3752669
E-mail: booknet@book.co.th
Distribution:
UK & Ireland: Paths International Ltd.
P O BOX 4083
Reading, Berkshire
RG8 8ZN
U.K.
E-mail: pathsmail@aol.com

Rest of the world: Booknet Co., Ltd.
1173, 1175, 1177, 1179 Srinakharin Road
Suan Luang, Bangkok 10250
Thailand
Tel: +66 2 3223678
Fax: +66 2 7211639
E-mail: booknet@book.co.th

Printed and bound in Thailand by
Amarin Printing & Publishing Public Company Limited

All rights reserved. No part of this publication may be reproduced, stored in a retrieval system, or transmitted in any form or by any means, electronic, mechanical, photocopying, recording or otherwise, without the prior permission of the publisher.

dos & don'ts in HONG KONG

dos
&
don'ts

CONTENTS

ACKNOWLEDGMENTS

The authors wish to acknowledge the
inestimable practical help and moral support
of the Leong and Storey families.
Our thanks also to Lucia Tsui, our favourite
consultant on all things Chinese.

Jon Hui is thanked for his comments
on the manuscript.

INTRODUCTION

HONG KONG

DO read on, we have some good advice for you!

DON'T be offended by some of our observations on life in Hong Kong and on the inhabitants of this great city. The three authors are a mixed bunch: one is a China-born Chinese lady, another is an English lady who has lived in China and Hong Kong for over thirty years and has been married to a Chinese gentleman for longer than that, and the third person is an English gentleman who has lived in Hong Kong for over fifteen years. We all work in local organisations and have all been classed as 'permanent Hong Kong residents' by the all-powerful Hong Kong Immigration Department, so that must mean something.

DO we know what we're talking about? Well, singly, each of us might be charged with particular prejudices and slants on what to expect in Hong Kong, but we have checked each other's work assiduously and left out anything that all three don't agree on.

So **DO** believe us when we say that we really love Hong Kong, even though it's a place to love and hate by turn. We love it because of the sheer excitement and vitality of almost 7 million people working hard to make a living on a group of a few islands, large and small. We love the place, even though sometimes it's too fast for its own good.

DON'T you wish Hong Kong were more 'fragrant' outside as well as inside the many perfume shops? Hong Kong means 'fragrant harbour', but you wouldn't know it if you breathed in deeply by the waterside. It is pretty polluted (in parts) and dirty (in parts). However, it shows such SPIRIT that

it's difficult not to come away with some sense of admiration for the people and their justifiable pride in the achievement of carving one of the greatest conurbations in the world out of a set of barren rocks. Well, not exactly - there were many settlements and a few thousand residents here long before the British arrived. Yes, our history goes back a good many thousand years.

So...if you're thinking of spending some time in Hong Kong (and the chances are, you are, otherwise why read this book?), then...

DON'T be put off by negative stories from friends and acquaintances. Hong Kong isn't wild like Tokyo or squeaky clean like Singapore (thank God). Nor is it as traffic-snarled as Bangkok.

So **DO** come and experience it for yourself and **DO** be ready to be captivated by a city of noise, glitter, breathtaking views - a unique part of the world which pulses with life.

Disclaimer....

(Don't authors of advice guides always put in something like this?)

We wrote most of this 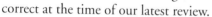 at some speed under some pressure (this is Hong Kong, after all... there is ALWAYS pressure) from mid 1999 to early 2000 - and then checked it all over again in mid-2004. All the information was, to the best of our knowledge, correct at the time of our latest review.

DON'T be too annoyed with us if a place we've mentioned has disappeared, changed its name or, like the ever-diminishing harbour, been filled in and built upon. Things move fast in Hong Kong (except democracy).

DON'T be put off this guide if a relative of the first Hong Kong Chief Executive, Tung Chee-hwa, has since gone off and married one of the last British Governor Chris Patten's daughters.

DON'T be surprised if on your first day here, something happens or someone says something which would entirely invalidate a statement in this book.

DO realise that this is HONG KONG, a place built upon tantalising contradictions, a place where any sweeping generalisation will immediately be undermined by an irritating exception. One example will suffice here: "Of course", insists a know-it-all Hong Kong expatriate, "Hong Kong people speak Cantonese, you know. But now that they are part of China again, they will probably ditch English as a second language in favour of the national Chinese dialect (Mandarin or putonghua)". The next day, that same expatriate stands in the McDonald's queue behind a Northern Chinese from the Mainland who is trying to order his fries in Mandarin and gets a reply from the 17-year old girl behind the counter: "If you don't know Cantonese, speak English please!"

DON'T think in terms of the whole of Hong Kong as one big mass of Chinese people, all with the same character, background and motivation. Hong Kong has long been a melting pot of a myriad nationalities and racial groups from Asia, Europe, North and South America, Australasia, the Middle East and even Africa. More especially, Hong Kong is the home to many different Chinese ethnic and language groupings.

Archaeological evidence and records show that the Hong Kong area of South China has been inhabited for more than four thousand years. Various groups of boat people probably came first. These are today's Tangka group, with the Hokklo coming from Swatow in the nineteenth century. The Punti (i.e. 'local' people) arrived somewhere around the tenth century AD and the Hakka in the seventeenth century.

You can still distinguish the Hakka women in the New Territory areas (and occasionally doing heavy work on

urban building sites) wearing traditional black *saam foo* - i.e. a Chinese-style jacket over trousers, and broad-rimmed straw hats trimmed with black fabric. However, the main ethnic grouping of Chinese is the *Han* Chinese who can be divided up into

many regional, language and clan groupings.

So a *Han* Shanghainese will have a slightly different attitude to life from a Hong Kong-born Chinese, and when we talk with one another (assuming we have a common spoken language) each will know where the other is coming from. So...

DO recognise that we Chinese not only have ideas of stereotypical behaviour of foreigners, we also have ingrained preconceptions about ourselves, our Chinese compatriots and the village, city or province of our birth.

The main difference in outlook on life can be seen between Northerners and Southerners. Beijing people are seen to be a little conservative, old fashioned, stiff, formal and polite, whereas we Cantonese (the vast majority of Hong Kong residents) regard ourselves as modern, smart, creative, worldly and ever so slightly rebellious where Northerners consider us crude, rude, over-boisterous, and difficult to control. This is borne out by history since most of the recent Chinese revolutions seem to have started in the South - a long way from the capital city.

Can we identify some major character traits of the Hong Kong Chinese? Well, as we've just said, generalisations are invidious, and there are many peoples around the world you could ascribe these traits to, but heck, here goes anyway:

Bad points

We're impatient. Look at us in a lift waiting for the doors to close. We'll press the 'close' button within seconds.

We're totally spatially unaware. We'll enter a lift or train before anyone can get out. We'll walk straight towards you because THAT'S where we're going, whether you're in the way or not. While walking in front of you,

we'll meander (our homes are small, so we prefer to wander the streets). We supposedly recoil from physical contact with strangers, but do an awful lot of it on the pavements and station platforms!

We're intolerant. If you're in the way, we will, albeit gently (mostly), physically push you aside.

If you're different, we'll avoid you. As a foreigner, you should get used to being the last person on a train we'll sit next to, unless there's a gay couple holding hands further down the carriage - in which case, you'll find the area around you very snug and crowded.

We're unwilling to confront a personal problem which may arise with another individual. Saying to most of us, "We have a problem. Can we talk about it, settle matters between us and move on?" will be answered (if at all) by a swift "There's no problem, (*mo man tai a!*) you're imagining it!" The whole exchange could prove very counter productive and the problem may remain unresolved for months.

We're insensitive and sometimes a bit too direct for comfort. If there's something wrong with someone, we'll stare. If somebody falls flat on their face after tripping on a banana skin, we'll laugh. You can walk into work one morning feeling good about your new hair-do, and one of us will say, "What have you done to your hair? I don't like it! It makes you look Korean!" Or, "Why is your face so red? Have you been drinking?"

We like every plan to be fully discussed and spelled out, before we take any action. This can sometimes take days, but...

Good points

We're quick, efficient and prompt. Once you've got to a situation where all parties have agreed on a plan, the task will be completed as fast or faster than anywhere else on earth.

We're immensely generous to family and friends. Whatever gift you give us will be reciprocated tenfold

at the next opportunity. You will not be able to 'ace' us with a superior gift. This is partly because we don't want to lose face, but also because of our sense of pride and pleasure in the very act of giving.

We're mostly very honest and law abiding. This is one of the safest cities in the world. The worst that can happen to you is having your pocket picked. If you give your car to a carhop for parking, you can leave small change in it and it'll probably be there when you get back (there have been some exceptions though!) The triad gangs will leave foreigners alone, but you may almost certainly be unwittingly donating money to their coffers if you do something on the borderline of legality.

DO learn at least one word of Cantonese! If we look solemn or act off-hand, it's usually because we're very apprehensive about speaking English, or we've had a previous bad experience with a ranting foreigner, or both. Try one word of Cantonese and the whole atmosphere will change. In 99 percent of cases, you'll be rewarded with a smile and a great deal of warmth.

After all this advice, our general message is

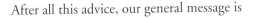

DON'T be surprised at what you find and **DON'T** ask your bookseller (or us) for your money back. We two *pang yau* (friends), your long suffering authors, know very well that if we say something is so, our fellow citizens will go out of their way to disprove it!

It goes with the territory.....

DO use the correct word to describe Hong Kong (or, as some people write it, 'Hongkong')...

DON'T call Hong Kong a colony...the Chinese communist government in Beijing (Peking) would take great exception to it... as would we proud citizens. Since July 1st, 1997, Hong Kong has been a Special Administrative Region (SAR) of the People's Republic of China (PRC). Just what an SAR is will be explained below.

DON'T call Hong Kong a territory. This used to be the politically correct way of describing the geographical area which was in fact a British colony. It is still in use, but is dying out.

DO be aware of the basics of Hong Kong history before you get here. It will give you a real perspective on what makes the place tick.

Historians have noted that Chinese people have a slightly different perspective on history than their counterparts in the West. Westerners' concepts of history are mostly based on big events and definite dates: 1066, 1777, etc. Chinese people think of all history as concertina-ed into one big 'yesterday'. Far off events still seem very fresh. Traditionally told and retold at grandmother's knee are tales of great battles and the victories of famous generals. The great classical (and classic) novels of China are read and re-read in many forms including comic books, reinforcing a pride in China's long-lived civilisation. So, for Chinese people, nineteenth century history seems like yesterday, and the pain and humiliation China felt as a 'sliced-up melon' of the Western colonial powers is as real today as yesterday. Historical wrongs are remembered forever.

Notwithstanding this, given the tendency of Westerners to view history as a long strand of consecutive events, visitors could do worse than remember a few important dates.

DO remember the basic dates of the history of the city of Hong Kong, and if you feel you need to know more than the basics below, **DO** read Jan Morris' *Hong Kong: Xianggang* (Viking, 1998), or Nigel Cameron's *An Illustrated History of Hong Kong* (Oxford University Press, 1991).

1842 The Treaty of Nanking (Nanjing). Great Britain gets Hong Kong Island 'in perpetuity' as reparation for Chinese 'aggression'. Chinese Governor Lin had tried to stop the appalling trade in opium by destroying a very large British consignment from India. Opium was the only thing the foreigners could find that we Chinese might crave for in return for the massive demand in Europe and America for silver, tea and porcelain. The people back in Britain thought their representatives in China had negotiated a lousy deal. Hong Kong was a dank, remote and disease-ridden set of rocks somewhere in the South China Sea. We Chinese, for our part, have felt shame about it ever since. This was the first of the 'unequal treaties', when the corrupt Qing emperors were too weak to stand up against the powerful foreign devils (*gwailos*). Until this happened, there was no concept of China, the 'Middle Kingdom', the centre of the world, ceding or giving up any territory belonging to the emperors, the sons of heaven. We have been known to shed tears talking about the sheer unfairness and immorality of Britain's actions, even today.

1860 The Convention of Peking *(Beijing)*. The Kowloon (nine dragons) peninsula is added to Hong Kong island as a British dependency.

1898 This date is really important, because it tells you everything you need to know about why Hong Kong was 'handed back' to China one hundred years later in 1997. On July 1st 1898, Britain was leased the New

Territories beyond Kowloon for ninety-nine years. So Britain had Hong Kong Island and part of the mainland - Kowloon - in perpetuity, but the New Territories were only on loan for the next century. This is why the subject of Hong Kong's future became a burning diplomatic issue in the early 1980s when the length of New Territories land leases could no longer be guaranteed for more than 15 years. If Britain couldn't keep the New Territories, the continuation of a British colony beyond the deadline for the lease was simply not a viable proposition.

1945 Liberation from the Japanese. The end to three years and eight months of Japanese occupation. (After the handover, the traditional public holiday for this was scrapped and lumped together with the Chung Yeung Festival).

1945-1951 Influx of refugees from the Mainland. The population increases from 600,000 to 2.36 million.

1949 Mainland China is taken over by the Chinese Communist Party (founded 1921). 'Liberation' is declared on October 1st, 1949, and the People's Republic of China is founded.

1967 Local patriots riot in Hong Kong in support of the Cultural Revolution of their Chinese compatriots over the border. The British government clamps down but becomes more aware of the need for a certain amount of social change.

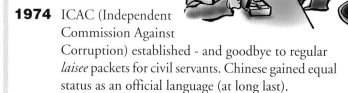

1974 ICAC (Independent Commission Against Corruption) established - and goodbye to regular *laisee* packets for civil servants. Chinese gained equal status as an official language (at long last).

1976 Workers granted a statutory day off every week (about time too). Before this, days off and holidays were deducted from workers' pay.

1978 Nine-years free education extended to junior secondary school (i.e., up to the third year of middle school).

1979 Hong Kong begins its rapid growth into one of Asia's miracle economic dragons as China opens up to the world under the leadership of Deng Xiaoping and his 'Four Modernisation' policy.

1982 District Board elections held for the first time - our first taste of (limited) democracy. Enter Margaret Thatcher. In a meeting with the Chinese paramount leader Deng Xiaoping in Beijing, it takes about three minutes for her to realise that China wants Hong Kong back; there was to be no alternative position, and certainly no discussion about the rights and wrongs of it. The only sensible way forward for Thatcher is to negotiate a smooth 'handover' smack in the middle of the year the New Territories lease runs out: July 1st, 1997.

1984 Signing of the Sino-British 'Joint Declaration' on the future of Hong Kong and its handover. A new 'constitution' for Hong Kong, horribly called a 'Basic Law' for the new 'Special Administrative Region' is 'promulgated'. Hong Kong is to be the flagship of Deng Xiaoping's seemingly unworkable idea of 'one country, two systems'. Hong Kong will carry on exactly as before for 50 years after the handover, with no interference from Beijing in its capitalist systems and way of life. This is greeted with some scepticism in Hong Kong and people begin to make plans to leave. The flight of the professional middle classes would spell doom for any continued economic miracle.

1989 The massacre of students and workers in Tiananmen in Beijing seems to confirm the pessimists' worst nightmares. How can the Chinese Communist Party tolerate any kind of *laissez-faire* economy and limited democracy in Hong Kong? More people make plans to leave. British governors begin to bring in more democracy, particularly Chris Patten (1992-1997) who increases the number of directly elected seats to the legislature without going through the formality of asking Beijing if it's OK to do so (they're not in charge yet, so it's none of their business). China reacts by going into a staged diplomatic sulk, delaying major infrastructure projects such as a new container terminal and the new airport.

1997 The 'Handover' (called 'The Return' in Chinese). It happens - a truly significant, and unusually, predictable historical event. The heavens open while the British flag is lowered and the festivities take place and we superstitious locals wonder if it's an omen. Foreigners down champagne as Prince Charles and a tearful Chris Patten sail away on *Britannia*. By now, there's a feeling amongst us that Beijing might stick to its word and leave Hong Kong alone - though the electoral reforms implemented by Patten are immediately scrapped by the leaders in Beijing, just as they said they would be. Tung Chee-hwa is set up as Hong Kong's first Chief Executive. People shelve their plans to leave. Quite a few Hong Kong migrants return home from Canada and Australia, only to be faced in 1998 with an Asian economic meltdown.

2002   In a blow to democracy lovers, Tung Chee-wha is 're-elected' for a second term by a small group of local bigwigs.

2003   The meltdown continues, encouraged by a wholly new viral strain called Severe Acute Respiratory Syndrome, or SARS for short. The fact that the name of this condition bears a close resemblance to the HKSAR (Hong Kong Special Administrative Region) acronym is not lost on a superstitious and suffering populace. On top of this come mass demonstrations against the Article 23 anti-subversion law, followed by resignation of two ministers in Tung's cabinet.

The story continues...read your daily newspapers or check out the *South China Morning Post* on the Web...

DO try to remember the names of a few important actors in this melodrama:

Deng Xiaoping *(1904-1997)*: China's former 'paramount' leader, one of the pantheon of Communist 'originals' who had been on the famed Communist Long March in the 1930s. He had hoped to visit Hong Kong after the Handover but never made it. It was he who started China on the road to a capitalist future. "It doesn't matter", he said, "whether a cat is black or white, as long as it catches mice!" In other words, to become a modern country, China would have to compromise some of its basic communist principles.

Chris Patten: Last Governor of Hong Kong , the showman, friend or foe, depending on whose side you're on, who withdrew to France to write his memoirs and later became an EU Commissioner, then Chancellor of Oxford University. An architect of the Conservative's UK election victory in 1992, he carelessly lost his own seat in Parliament in the process. Some say he was given Hong Kong as a consolation prize. Signs are that history will be kinder to him; many Hong Kong people quite liked him because he seemed genuine enough and wasn't afraid to stand up to China. He was the first real politician (as opposed to diplomat) to occupy the position of Governor, so when Beijing called him "son of a cur", he surprised them all by laughing it off as quite a compliment compared to the usual Western tabloid epithets.

Tung Chee-hwa: The first Chief Executive of the Hong Kong Special Administrative Region. He is in charge of an SAR which is part of China, but supposedly autonomous in all but foreign affairs. A kindly, avuncular, elderly man, given the post after a non-election by 400 of Hong Kong's 'finest' citizens (all nominated by Beijing). He has a really difficult job trying to maintain any independence of action, particularly as Beijing bailed his ailing shipping company out in the 1980s. His term of office has been plagued by worrying misfortunes, such as the airport opening fiasco, the economic turmoil, the SARS epidemic, anti-subversion law demonstrations and the closure of innumerable cake shops. Reappointed for a second term in 2002.

Anson Chan: Tung Chee-hwa's, and before that, Chris Patten's deputy as Chief Secretary of the Hong Kong civil service. An important person in giving a sense of continuity and stability beyond British rule. Tainted in the communists' eyes by her association with the Imperialists, she has maintained her dignity in adversity. But some saw her as another Ci Xi (last Empress of China, with a reputation for ruthlessness). She stood down in early 2001 amid much gossip that the Beijing leadership was giving her a very hard time, and was replaced by Donald Tsang, former Financial Secretary noted for his bow ties.

Zhang Zemin: Former President of China. The panda on the podium who got the keys to Hong Kong on July 1st, 1997. The first Communist Chinese leader with a taste for showmanship, a Presidential style, and an eye on the foreign media. Stepped down in March 2003 but as head of China's Military Commission remains the power behind the throne.

Zhu Rongji: Former Prime Minister of China. The tough guy economist, not afraid to call the shots against corrupt officials and ailing state enterprises. Retired in 2003 to make way for a new generation of younger leaders in their 60s.

Hu Jintao: Latest President of China and head of the Chinese Communist Party, and

Wen Jiabao: Latest Prime Minister of China. Visited Hong Kong in mid-2003 and won some hearts and minds by visiting Amoy Gardens, the housing estate most badly affected by the SARS epidemic.

Both are still unknown quantities but hope springs eternal that they will usher in a new age in Chinese politics - even though they rose through the ranks of a Party known more for interminable conformist disquisition than for being a hotbed of bold and innovative (read 'democratic') political debate. Still, the sacking of major Party figures for incompetence during the Beijing SARS outbreak of 2003 may herald a move towards more responsive and responsible government.

Li Peng: Arch-conservative in the Chinese Communist party, associated in everyone's mind with the Tiananmen events of June 1989 and the mega Three Gorges Dam project...the less said about him the better.

DON'T come to Hong Kong thinking that the place is one built-up mess of high-rises, skyscrapers and department stores. Nine tenths, yes, nine tenths of Hong Kong is green.

DO take time to go out of the city into the New Territories, or even up the Peak on Hong Kong Island - and you will see that the place can be really wild. We've got a city zoological gardens, but, in addition, just a few yards off the highway in the country parks (there are lots of them, and there's even a bird sanctuary) lurk monkeys and poisonous snakes (nine varieties, including cobra). Two of the authors have never seen a free-roaming snake, but one has seen cobras, yellow-banded

kraits, and bamboo snakes - all in the urban areas. Anyway, you are sure to see them in the shops in the Western District and Sham Shui Po where live snakes are stripped of their gall bladders for medicinal purposes.

DON'T go to a snake shop if you are squeamish or a lover of our reptilian friends.

So what constitutes the spot on this planet called Hong Kong?

HONG KONG is actually the island of Hong Kong, and is called 'Hong Kong side' as opposed to Kowloon which is called

'Kowloon side'. Hong Kong Island used to have a capital called Victoria. No-one uses the name now, and this main central business district of Hong Kong (Island) is called, predictably, CENTRAL. ADMIRALTY is where the British fleet used to park itself, and it's just east of Central. WESTERN is at the western end of the harbour, and the EASTERN corridor is on the east of the Island. The PEAK is a hill above Central where all the bigwigs live and where you can take snapshots of the sweeping vistas of the whole of the Hong Kong skyline. CAUSEWAY BAY and STANLEY are shopping areas on the Island. So far, so easy, eh?

DON'T be put off by the Chinese names everywhere. Many of them are translated into English and there are bi-lingual Chinese/English signs all over the place, including street signs, train and bus stops, etc. So the Chinese characters, pronounced 'Jungwaan', are also displayed as 'Central'. But...

You **DO** have to learn some Chinese place names, such as WANCHAI, the late-night entertainment district on the Island. And there are many more Chinese names to learn once you board the Star Ferry at Central and five minutes later arrive at Kowloon. Kowloon is a peninsula of the mainland mass of China pointing south at the Island. The first landmark after the Star Ferry, is, yes, you guessed it, the Peninsula Hotel, and

starting its run north for miles alongside it is Nathan Road.

DON'T expect any names like Ho Chi Minh Boulevard (yet). Fears that the Chinese government would rename Nathan Road 'East is Red Avenue' have proved unfounded so far, although the former HMS Tamar barracks, now home to the People's Liberation Army Hong Kong Garrison, has been renamed 'Central Barracks'. Government House was also given a new, supposedly Chinese name but nobody seems to use it as it is still called 'Government House' in both English and Chinese. All the major roads of Hong Kong are still called after colonial governors, some good, some bad, some indifferent: Nathan, Bowring, Lugard, Stubbs, Des Voeux...the list goes on and on.

But **DO** try and get your tongue around the area of Kowloon bordering the harbour which is full of restaurants, hotels and shops: it's called TSIM SHA TSUI - and it's a REALLY difficult three words to get right. Try, as near as dammit, 'JIM SA JOI' with the taxi driver and see where it gets you (Mexico probably!). Most expats rely on 'TST', and some Australasians call it 'Jimsy', but they would, wouldn't they?

So now you're in Kowloon. A walk up Nathan Road will take you ever deeper into shopping territory.

DO remember to wear sensible shoes. Nathan Road is VERY

long. It's best seen at twilight when all the neon signs are illuminated. If you keep travelling straight north, you will eventually be walking uphill towards the LION ROCK and the 'Nine Dragons' range (*gau* = nine, *lung* = dragon = Kowloon). This line of hills forms the barrier between Kowloon and the New Territories. Most people travel over it by car or bus, or under it by car or bus or train through the Lion Rock tunnel. Catch the Lion Rock at the right angle - to your right just as you come out of the road or rail tunnels into the New Territories - and it looks like a lion (and curiously, a mixture of a British lion and a Chinese lion).

Now you're in the New Territories. If you continue northwards travelling by car or train for about 30 minutes through places like SHA TIN, TAI PO, TAI WO, FAN LING and SHEUNG SHUI - all sleepy villages not so long ago, now vast new towns - you will eventually get to the Chinese border at LO WU. Lo Wu and other crossing points remain exactly like any border crossing to a foreign country. Entry into the SAR by mainland Chinese citizens, and into Shenzhen by travellers from Hong Kong, is still rigorously controlled.

On the way, you will have seen how green and hilly and full of islands most of Hong Kong is and just how extensive.

DON'T be surprised that Hong Kong is anything BUT just a couple of rocks with some buildings on them.

DO hike along the trails in the country parks. The views are spectacular and you'll come across all sorts of interesting historical temples and villages and even an ancient cannon or two. The Hong Kong Tourism Board offices will have all the details.

DON'T be fooled into thinking that all of Hong Kong is developed and full of people. Hikers have been known to die of exposure or have been burnt to death by hill fires up on the mountains. It can be very lonely and the weather can be very treacherous up there.

So when off hiking, **DO** tell someone where you're going, and **DO** take a mobile phone (and make sure it will work in outlying areas).

DON'T be too afraid though. Sadly the last wild Hong Kong tiger was shot by hunters in Fanling in the early 1900s. But there are snakes, a few wild boar, civet cats and other endangered species out there still.

You can hike on the Maclehose Trail (named after another British governor) that crosses from east to west, inlet to inlet. The very fit amongst us have races along this trail every year. A normal team of four people manages to traverse the trail in about 20 to 24 hours non-stop. When they were here with the British army, the Ghurkas always used to win because they could do it in 11! This hike is not for the faint of heart, but you can do it in short stages. It's an excellent way to get some spectacular views over the islands, paddle at the seaside, fill your tired lungs with fresh air, and finish the day with copious amounts of noodles, fried rice and beer in the village cafes along the way.

A NOTE ON
CHINESE NAMES

Personal names

DO remember the simple rule that the surname comes first. But...

DO bear in mind that it's not as simple as that. First, the given name follows the surname. The given name is usually two characters - in practice, two syllables - separated by a dash. We don't like the northern Chinese practice of a single character/ syllable for a given name; it's not poetic enough, and probably a bit common. Thus, in Hong Kong:

MISS CHEUNG WAI-MING

Miss...

(where Cheung is the surname, and Wai-ming is the given name)

DON'T call a person by his/her given name unless you're invited to. The given name is VERY personal, and is only used by family and VERY close friends.

So, in the case above, it's Ms Cheung to you. But to get over this difficulty, and attesting to the fact that Hong Kong has a long history of association with foreigners, we have tended to be given or to give ourselves 'Western' or 'Christian' forenames. There has been a long tradition of nuns in missionary schools assigning Western names to secondary school pupils (there was usually no choice in this matter - the names were biblical and, in many cases, slightly old-fashioned - e.g. Enoch, Eliza, Benedict, Joshua, Gladys, Edith). So:

EDITH Cheung Wai-ming

Yes, **DO** call her Edith, if you know her well enough.

DON'T get complacent though, it gets even more complicated - particularly with Hong Kong women. We married ladies tend to retain our maiden and husband's surnames, but still use our maiden name (and maiden status) in day-to-day business. Thus:

Edith WONG Cheung Wai-ming
(where Miss Cheung married a Mr. Wong).

So, DO call her Miss (yes, Miss) Edith Cheung, and don't mention or bother to dwell on her married status.

As a bit of light relief from all this, perhaps you'd like to peruse the following. **DO** believe us when we say that all the examples of 'Christian' forenames listed below have been seen around town from badges in fast food restaurants to items in the newspaper. The names have (sometimes) been scrambled to protect the innocent, but the forenames are real. The younger the person, it seems, the more outrageous the name...signs of rebellion amongst our teen generation (especially the girls who choose very interesting names)?

MALE	**FEMALE**
Crusader Wong	Suburbia Yau
G-force Lau	Bibiana Lu
Silent Pang	Vulva Yu
Fenkins Lee	Pheon Kwok
Jones Poon	Sicily Won
Eddo So	Winki Wei
Belly Yim	Moonique Chu
Rambo To	Rainbow Fung
Mustang Chang	Chlorine Lam
Crusher Choi	Chrystallite Yip
Napoleon Wong	Milky Wei
Polaris Pun	Amoeba Au
Banky Choi	Ronky Wu
Cozy Lau	Jelly Chan
Hitler Ho	Apple Pan

DON'T be surprised if your office assistant suddenly decides to change her chosen Western forename. If it's not registered with the Hong Kong government, it can be changed at will. The person you've been calling Monica for three years might walk in one Monday morning and tell you she's now called Nicole because she's crazy about Nicole Kidman's new film.

Our Chinese names are normally chosen by grandparents or our parents so **DO** be prepared for most of them to have very significant meanings. They usually involve lofty aspirations and some of us are even named in the hope of what the next child will (or won't) be, e.g., Oi Dai (love a younger brother) or Yau Ling (the youngest, i.e., definitely the last one, we hope).

Amongst ourselves, we often call each other by our surnames as a familiar form of address, so **DON'T** be surprised if a Mr Cheng is called 'Cheng' by his friends. Or we may be called by the second syllable of our given name preceded by 'Ah', e.g. Ah Fai, Ah Ling. This is often the way we address our household helpers, e.g., Ah Jing, Ah Fung, but to be more respectful yet still friendly we may say Jing Jie, Fung Jie (Jie = elder sister). **DON'T** be afraid to follow suit.

...Jie

唔該

(excuse me)

Nicknames are also common amongst friends and gangs and they are often quite direct and unkind. **DON'T** be shocked to hear a fat person being called 'Fatty Pang' or someone with bad skin being called 'Pock-Marked Wong'.

Within the family, designations are very complicated but very precise. Family members have an exact designation, depending on their specific relationship within the family. These designations are used in everyday conversation in preference to actual names. For example, we will call our eldest sister *'Ga Jie'* and younger brother *'Dai Dai'*. Our maternal grandmother is *'Popo'* and paternal grandfather, *'Yeh Yeh'*. A female cousin older than ourselves is *'Biu Jie'*, a male cousin younger than ourselves is *'Biu Dai'*. Our elder brother's wife is *'Ah So'*. Out of respect, we address people we don't really know, such as hawkers and workmen, in a similar way, e.g., *Ah Sum*, (younger auntie), *Ah Po* (grandma), *Ah Suk* (younger uncle), *Ah Baak* (grandpa) depending on how old we are ourselves. **DON'T** hesitate to do the same.

Company names

Companies will similarly go for names with lofty aspirations, many of which reflect competitive money-mad Hong Kong culture.

DO expect names in Cantonese to lead to some humorous and unfortunate transliterations into English, especially when the word for store or small business - *kee* (pronounced *gay* in Cantonese, but read as *key* in English by the innocent observer) - is used.

DON'T be surprised to find that the following are genuine company names in Hong Kong (Chinese meanings in brackets where appropriate):

- Lofty Virtue Publishing Company
- Big Profit Finance Co
- The Best Restaurant
- Never Second Company
- Lucky Funeral Parlour
- Hang On Curtain Co ('Happy Peace' Curtain Co)
- Wong Kee Furniture Factory (Wong's Furniture Factory)
- Chung Kee Jewellery Company (Chung's Jewellery Company)

- Tacky Garment Co ('Virtuous' Garment Co)
- Lee Kee Boat Co (Lee's Boat Co)
- Healthy Mess restaurant
- Hop On Bicycle Co. (United Peace Bicycle Co)
- Mee See Shoe Shop (Missy Shoe Shop)

Property names

The same goes for buildings. **DON'T** be astonished to find that drab blocks of highrises wedged in between dozens of others bear some stunning and surprising names:

- Palatial Crest
- Hollywood Heights
- Pacific Palisades
- Onward Building
- Cheerful Commercial Building
- Golden Mansion

But one of the most unfortunate choices of all:

The Belcher's (situated on a road named after former Colonial Governor Belcher)

GETTING IN,
ROUND AND ABOUT,
AND OUT

We've already said something about getting oriented to the basic geography of Hong Kong. Let's go on now to the nitty-gritty of getting into the SAR in the first place and what to expect when you arrive here.

Arriving by air

You **DON'T** believe your luck do you? You've arrived at one of the most modern airports in the world. All that acreage of carpet! Someone must have made a packet out of it! The Airport is properly entitled the 'Hong Kong International Airport', but in Hong Kong, we call it after the island that was flattened to accommodate it: Chep Lap Kok - now rapidly being shortened to 'CLK'. The airport was opened in 1998 and there were a few (*ahem*) teething problems, particularly with the cargo system (locally known as the Chek Lap Kokup!). Now all that's been sorted out, and we have an airport we can be proud of. But if you've been to Hong Kong before and have been used to the old tiny airport at Kai Tak, with its stunningly gut-wrenching roof-top right turn to find the runway...

DON'T be disappointed with CLK - there are magnificent views of the islands before landing, and, depending on the direction the plane takes, a breathtaking sweep around the whole of Hong Kong Island and the Central District.

You get off the plane and head down the travelators (very long travelators sometimes). You may even have to get on the driverless train if your plane parks at one of the very distant gates. Press on anyway till you get to the Immigration Hall. You will probably have filled in an arrivals card on the airplane. Line up at the appropriate counter (e.g., 'Visitors').

You then proceed to the baggage hall. Here there are toilets, a Hong Kong Tourism Board counter (free literature and offers during your stay!) and free courtesy phones for local calls.

DO check the information displayed over the baggage carousel so you know which exit to use for the arrival hall: A or B? This is important if someone's meeting you, because the arrival hall is very long and narrow, and you need to come out at the right (or left) end.

Head for Customs with your baggage.

DO note that all the usual VERY strict penalties apply for importing illegal drugs, too much alcohol and tobacco, and pornographic literature (interestingly, while English speakers call porn 'blue', the Chinese call it 'yellow').

You are now in the arrival hall. Most of the information about what to do next can be found in the centre. There you will find exits to all the various forms of transport.

DO beware of touts and pickpockets. As we've noted, Hong Kong is a relatively safe place to be, but you never can be too careful.

DON'T accept lifts from touts offering cheap transport to the city.

To get to the business end of Hong Kong, you will need to travel over and through the magnificent bridges and tunnels separating Lantau (the biggest island of Hong Kong) from Kowloon and Hong Kong Island. There's plenty of transport to choose from at the airport.

Permission to stay

If you are going to stay in Hong Kong for any length of time, **DO** check your entrance visa for the length of stay the immigration official stamped on your passport. You will have to report to the Immigration Department for any alteration in stay and status.

If you want to work here and were not recruited abroad by government or business, you will need a work permit from the Immigration Department.

DO allow one whole day for any visit to Immigration Tower in Gloucester Road, Central. The Department now has computer-controlled hotlines for making appointments, but you NEVER know how long the process will take (you will have to give a thumbprint and have your photograph taken, etc.).

DO take with you every document that ever had anything to do with your life, and photocopies of them as well. They won't require your inside leg measurement, but if you don't have the relevant document, you will be forced to make another appointment and lose another day.

Hotel courtesy buses/limousines

DO report to the hotel information counter at the centre of the arrivals hall.

Taxis

DON'T expect a 10-minute taxi ride into the centre of Hong Kong. CLK is quite a long way out from Hong Kong and Kowloon on Lantau Island. It takes at least 30 minutes to Hong Kong Island.

DO make sure that the taxi driver puts the flag down to start the meter when you set off.

DO remember that at the end of the journey, the driver will add on charges for baggage and tunnel/ bridge fees which you will have to pay (including, sometimes, the RETURN tunnel fee as well). This is all within the law. Also, because taxi fare schedules are revised upwards with monotonous regularity, the driver may refer you to a card hanging off his dash-board itemising the new charges, because his meter hasn't been unsealed, reset and resealed by officialdom yet. **DO** check the Hong Kong Tourism Board web site, 'All About Hong Kong - Useful Info - Getting Around' link, for detailed information on taxi fares.

Taxi drivers will issue receipts on request but **DO** ask BEFORE they put up the flag otherwise the data will be gone.

DO remember the colours of the taxis:

> RED taxis serve the urban areas;
> GREEN taxis serve the New Territories;
> BLUE taxis serve Lantau.

DON'T worry if you don't know where you're going, the guys in uniform at the taxi ranks will help you.

DO note a few other unique features about Hong Kong taxis:

• Taxi drivers pay an absolute fortune for the taxi license (millions of dollars). They can mortgage themselves for life for one.

• Taxis therefore spend 24 hours on the road (with shift drivers we hope) to get the best value for money.

• The boot (trunk) of a taxi may therefore be full of buckets, spare parts and rags, seemingly leaving zero room for your luggage. This is to ensure the taxi spends as long on the road as possible earning money.

• Taxi drivers always somehow miraculously manage to get your luggage safely stowed.

• Taxi drivers (well, many drivers) in Hong Kong like to have a nice perfume bottle stuck on their dashboard, and, for some reason, a calendar as well.

So, **DO** be assured that you may not know where you are going, but you will know the date on which you're travelling. This may be important if you're heavily jet-lagged!

Buses

There are airport buses which go to all parts of the SAR. They're comfortable and fast (the airport buses with the prefix A are slightly faster than those with the prefix E).

DO note that buses in Hong Kong don't give change. You pay a fixed fare which is displayed on entry and you put the money straight in the box by the driver. It's the same fare however long you stay on the bus. There are several competing bus companies, but the fares

and routes are all regulated by the government. The route network is very extensive, and can be found on some tourist maps.

DON'T expect us to get up from our seats for the elderly, the infirm or the pregnant. Our elderly stand in Hong Kong and let their dear grandchildren sit down. Our kids get top priority.

DON'T forget, this is Hong Kong, so the buses have unique features as well as the taxis:
• the big buses are mostly double-deckers (the British influence).
• many are air-conditioned and these cost more than non-airconditioned buses. (**DON'T** be stuck in a non-airconditioned

bus, in a traffic jam, in a tunnel, in August - you will expire from oxygen starvation and heat exhaustion)
• buses that go through tunnels have RED numbers on the front (except the fancy new ones with electronic displays). The first

of the three numbers denotes the tunnel the bus is going through (e.g., a 170 goes through '1', the Cross-Harbour tunnel, the 670 goes through the Eastern tunnel, and the 970 goes through the Western tunnel).

• the numbers of buses have letters after them, denoting they are going somewhere useful (e.g., 69M goes to an MTR station; a 310K goes to a KCR station - see below for what MTR and KCR mean).

DO go round Hong Kong Island by bus. A bus to Stanley from Central (under the Stock Exchange), a look around Stanley Market, and another bus round the rest of the Island is a great way to experience Hong Kong.

Anywhere round Lantau Island, and Tai Mo Shan and Route Twisk in the New Territories are great by bus too.

Minibuses

There are red and green minibuses which carry a maximum of 16 people (standing not allowed). Many of these can stop anywhere to pick up or disgorge passengers. They are very fast, and the fare is displayed on the windscreen in Arabic numbers and Chinese 'market' numbers (they're different from ordinary Chinese characters for numbers).

DO expect drivers to:
• talk or sing opera to themselves.

• complain about passengers long after they've alighted because they didn't shout loud enough or soon enough that they wanted to get off the bus.

• make and take calls on their portable phones (this must be done hands-free or, since mid-2000, they will be breaking the law).

• screech to a sudden halt because a potential passenger has been spotted.

DO shout '*YAU LOK*', or, 'STOP PLEASE' loudly and well in advance when you want to get off.

Trams

While we're on about buses, **DON'T** miss a tram ride between Happy Valley and Western on the Island. They're old, cranky and clanky, but a beautiful, cheap way to see Hong Kong.

DO sit upstairs to enjoy the views!

DO remember that trams are the exact opposite to buses: you get on the tram AT THE BACK and you pay the fixed fare when you leave AT THE FRONT!

DON'T forget you can hire a tram for a unique private party. Meandering through Wanchai on a Tram full of beer could be just the theme party you've been looking for. Call the tram company or your travel agent and they will arrange it for you!

DO take the Peak Tram. You can get a free open-topped bus from outside the City Hall Star Ferry in Central to the Peak Tram Station and then go up on the tram to the top and the newish shopping complex.

DO get a single up to the Peak on the Peak Tram, then come back down by road on a double-decker bus (the older the better) sitting in the front seat on the top deck. We can guarantee a rollicking ride down to Causeway Bay or Central. Definitely yet another way to experience Hong Kong.

Rickshaws (yes, Rickshaws)

DON'T take a red rickshaw ride from Star Ferry Central without negotiating with the 102-year old puller first. You'll get a very short ride round the block amongst the traffic and stared at by locals for being an 'imperialist lackey' from the old colonial days.

DO expect the old puller to pop his clogs (i.e., pass away) at any moment. In fact, our advice is, yes, pay for a photo of yourself sitting in the rickshaw, but,

DON'T travel in one.

Trains

The train station and ticket machines are in the centre of the arrival hall at the airport. The airport express train will take you to Hong Kong Island or Kowloon with only one or two stops. It's ultra-modern, clean, and very fast (20 - 30 minutes).

DO bear in mind that there are THREE train systems in Hong Kong:

• MASS TRANSIT RAILWAY (MTR). This is the one you will catch at the airport. It's mostly an underground, metro type system serving the urban areas.

• KOWLOON/CANTON RAILWAY (KCR). A surface rail going from central Kowloon next to the Cross-Harbour tunnel to Lo Wu at the border with the Chinese mainland, and, if you're on the right train, all the way to Canton (Guangzhou), Shanghai or Beijing.

• LIGHT RAIL TRANSIT (LRT). A surface system running way out in the New Territories.

In most cases, you can buy a ticket to your destination and travel on the MTR and KCR systems with the same ticket.

DON'T eat, drink or sit on floors in trains - you could be fined.

Do you want to save time and money? **DO** buy an OCTOPUS!

An Octopus ticket is a stored value card which allows you to travel on buses, minibuses and trains without diving into your pocket to find the right change. You just dump your wallet or handbag (with the card inside) on top of the sensor on the turnstile when entering or leaving and technology does the rest. You can load more money onto the card ($50 or more) at machines in the train stations.

Boats and ships - well ferries really

Ferries used to be the only way to travel from Hong Kong to Kowloon and from island to island. Now there are tunnels and bridges everywhere, but the ferries are still vital for many who live an island life in places like Discovery Bay ('Disco Bay' - a residential development far from the madding crowd.)

DO go by Star Ferry Central/Kowloon - the best value ride in Hong Kong with magnificent harbour views.

DO go to Cheung Chau or Lamma or Lantau from the Outlying Islands Ferry Pier at least once during your stay. A one hour ferry ride will take you to Cheung Chau where there are NO cars. You can have seafood from the English menu - with prices significantly more than we pay from our Chinese menus, but who cares? It's still a cheap and lovely day staring at the harbour and scoffing garlic prawns and Yeungchow fried rice.

DO hire a ferry for a private party. Contact the ferry companies or your travel agent.

Better still, **DO** go on a free JUNK junket with any friend who works for a Hong Kong multinational. All big companies seem to keep a motor-boat (no sails), locally called a junk, for entertaining customers by taking them out around the bays of the islands for swimming and good sea food at the waterside restaurants. The boats are usually very well appointed, are crewed and have on-board fridges full of beer and soft drinks. Yes, and they have toilets.

DO consider a boat or hydrofoil trip to China. You will still need to go through Immigration there and back and you will need a China visa.

DO get your China visa from a China Travel Service Office, or better still, from the Chinese Ministry of Foreign Affairs Office in China Resources Building, Harbour Road, Wanchai (it's cheaper there).

You can spend 2 days on a ship and sail up the China coast avast on the South China Sea to Shanghai from the China Ferry terminal in Kowloon. **DO** get the train back to Kowloon from Shanghai (travel hard class if you want to - but China is tiring enough without this particular form of backpacker masochism - whatever the tougher form of guidebooks urge you).

DO consider going to Macao, the former Portuguese enclave until its return to China in1999. But that's probably another book in this series...

Getting about by car

DO you really want to drive in Hong Kong? It's marginally safer than being a pedestrian. Traffic moves slowly, but cars jump in and out of virtual spaces in traffic queues as if they're made of elastic. There are fast roads, if you want to drive at 3 a.m. and dodge the 23-year-old road-racers in

their souped-up Hondas (some of us stay up all night on bridges to watch them). The new roads and flyovers seemingly jutting out into outer space do make Hong Kong a spectacular place to drive at times.

We don't have much of a car-hire culture. The transport systems are so good, you may not need one. You will probably only buy a car if you're intending to stay here long enough.

DO check with the Department of Transport about the validity of your overseas license. If the Department lets you drive on a foreign license, there will be a time limit.

Foreigners usually wind up buying the old (i.e., over 4 years) cars we don't want. We like expensive cars, the newer the better, with leather interiors, in metallic colours only, preferably silver or gold. We like distinctive number plates as well but...

DON'T get involved in local numerology, it will cost you a fortune, or you'll become hopelessly superstitious. Want to buy the number plate '8' for your car? Have you got a few million US dollars to take your chances in an auction (sometimes held by the Government for charity)? And you can't buy '1' - it's the Chief Constable's number.

How about '4444'? Well, you're welcome to it, as it's an incredibly unlucky number (the same sound as the word for 'death' in Chinese). No-one will touch it here.

DON'T expect to see many rusty cars in Hong Kong, except those driven by foreigners or on the car-wrecking tips in the New Territories.

DON'T be surprised if there seem to be more taxis in Hong Kong than people.

DON'T be surprised if there seem to be more BMW's and MERC's in Hong Kong than taxis.

DON'T argue with a policeman if you're stopped for speeding (or stopped for anything)!

DO carry your ID card and driving license at all times.

DO read the Highway Code.

DON'T expect to pass the Hong Kong driving test first go.

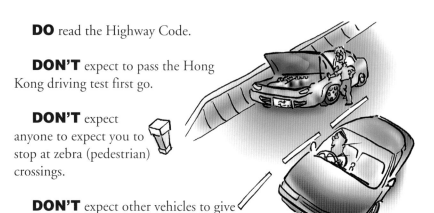

DON'T expect anyone to expect you to stop at zebra (pedestrian) crossings.

DON'T expect other vehicles to give way.

DON'T count on a vehicle turning in the direction of its indicator. Well, **DON'T** expect drivers to use their indicators at all (they waste the battery).

DON'T expect anyone to help in breakdowns and accidents (although we will stop and stare).

DO join the Hong Kong Automobile Association (the AA) for breakdown services.

If you break down, **DO** jam a dirty piece of newspaper out of the boot (trunk). Others (including policemen) will know you've broken down and are not trying to park illegally.

DON'T park ANYWHERE! If there are no markings on the road, it means you can't park there. If there are yellow lines on the road, it too means you can't park there. If it says 'PARKING', you probably can't park there either, unless you're driving an ambulance. There are parking areas but many of the spaces may be reserved for trucks, minibuses, visitors to an organisation, cars that have rented spaces monthly, emergency vehicles, rubbish collection vehicles, taxis, etc. The private car is being squashed off the roads as far as possible.

DO take your car into a pay car park or a parking meter bay. These can be quite expensive by the hour. The car park SHROFF (What? Please see the glossary elsewhere in the book) is where you pay for your ticket, before you leave the car park. This process tells you why it costs so much to park a car in Hong Kong, since it can involve 2 or 3 car-park staff just to get you out of the place.

DO expect only God to help you if you have to buy or rent a parking space. It will cost you the price of a house anywhere else in the world.

DON'T expect any sympathy from the Hong Kong government about the lack of facilities for owning a car in Hong Kong. Annual road taxes and new car import duties are deliberately and seemingly prohibitively high to discourage further growth of car ownership on Hong Kong's crowded roads. But, quite simply, they don't discourage anyone, since the more expensive it is for a family to get a new car on the road, the higher the status. It's the equivalent of paying the extra for an Amex gold card. Everyone has a gold or platinum card...it's too 'common' to have an ordinary green one (though, this being Hong Kong, it's more 'common' to have a gold one).

Leaving

DON'T forget to pay all your taxes before you leave. Income tax is due in one big bill once a year; depending on how much you earn, it can be huge.

DON'T worry, you can get quick tax loans from the Banks, but **DO** check for competitive interest rates.

Accommodation

DO check with the Hong Kong Tourism Board for accommodation deals in Hong Kong.

If you're staying in a hotel, **DO** book a package as part of your airfare, it is MUCH cheaper. Hotel walk-in rates can be prohibitive. Booking on the internet can also be cheaper.

DO note that Hong Kong has some of the best hotels in the world, like the Peninsula and the Mandarin Oriental. Travellers searching for a good economy deal usually go to the YMCA or YWCA hotels which are clean and comfortable. Backpackers with no budget at all end up in Chungking Mansions in Nathan Road, Kowloon. This is a rabbit-warren of cheap hotels, bordellos and fine Indian restaurants. If you can stand the filth in the stairwells, you should be OK - in the Indian restaurants anyway....

So, **DO** remember that Hong Kong has a range of accommodation from those offering supreme luxury to absolute dives.

GENERAL DOS
AND DON'TS

HONG KONG

Hong Kong is a city alive with street life. If you walk round the back streets you'll see at first hand how we residents live our lives on our doorsteps, working, gossiping, and watching the world go by. Street life has migrated even to public housing estates where you'll find our front doors wide open to the corridors with only a wrought iron gate between you and our family activities within. You'll also come across the flicker and noise of television sets, kept on all day as often as not, enticing smells of cooking, and the noise of *mahjong* tiles, loud ebullient voices, and giggling kids.

DO wander around and have a look for yourselves.

DON'T be shocked at where we live or how small our homes are. The majority of us live in apartments which may have to accommodate several generations of family members. The first government housing allocated the same square footage per person for living space as was standard for storage space in the UK. Our homes tend to be in multi-storey blocks in densely populated housing estates. Sometimes we might be lucky if the estate has a landscaped area with a swimming pool.

But **DO** be prepared for estates to be overcrowded and dilapidated, although we get magnificent views if we live on a high floor and there's almost certainly a market, restaurant and shopping centre conveniently nearby.

DON'T be amazed to see people's washing hanging out of windows on poles or even strewn over railings by the roadside. We like drying our clothes in the open air in Hong Kong.

And **DON'T** be surprised at the cost of our residences. Despite the economic downturn over the last few years, the prices of Hong Kong real estate are amongst the highest in the world and much of our government's budget surplus has come from the sale of land.

DO remember that we pay great attention to dress, appearance and behaviour and we will judge you on how you look and behave. We like to dress up in smart suits and ties, dresses and jewellery. Our men prefer to be clean-shaven and have short, neatly cut hair.  They usually look very dapper. Our women tend to dress well, use cosmetics and often look very smart with their neat trim figures.

DON'T be taken aback by the smell of mothballs mingled with expensive perfumes. We store our winter garments with overdoses of naphthalene.

DON'T expect us to ever look our age. Many of us remain lean and sinuous well into middle age. Moreover, our skin doesn't wrinkle very easily, and it often looks as though we have the secret of eternal youth.

We generally behave very well in public and don't like to be offensive or draw attention to ourselves by dressing outrageously or showing off in some way or other. There are exceptions (and it's often foreigners) but **DO** expect to feel different if you don't follow our local practice. Whatever else you do, **DO** wear proper footwear to smart restaurants, functions, concerts etc. If in doubt, **DON'T** ever wear flip-flops except to the beach or on other really informal occasions.

DON'T be offended if we ask you personal questions such as how much you earn, how much something costs or how old you are. This is quite normal here but **DO** just smile and look mysterious if you don't want to answer. **DON'T** take it badly either when we say we could have bought something cheaper elsewhere when you think you got it for a bargain.

DON'T expect all that many of us to be able to speak English or other foreign languages very well, and do speak clearly to us. Cantonese is the first language of the majority although some of us speak an interesting Hong Kong version of Chinglish in which English words are sprinkled into a Cantonese conversation.

DON'T forget that the force that drives us is making money. This is what gives our city its lustre, its relentless sense of purpose, its excitement, endless energy and at times manic frenzy. We're known to be workaholics and work long hours for our money.

DO expect to find our city full of nouveaux riches and **DON'T** worry about the attention paid to status symbols, designer labels and smart cars (MERCs, BMWs, Porsches and Rolls Royces - even though there's nowhere much to drive).

Because our houses are small and crowded we like to take guests out to Chinese restaurants to eat. But if we're better off we'll probably take you to a club such as the Hong Kong Club or the Jockey Club. We like spending our leisure time eating or relaxing in clubs, so **DON'T** be surprised to be invited out to eat all the time by your local friends, colleagues or business associates. And **DO** reciprocate our hospitality by inviting us back for a similar meal.

Nine years free education (to secondary school form 3) wasn't introduced until 1978 so **DON'T** be surprised to find that many of our older residents are illiterate or left school at a very early age. School is tough for our kids as they're given mountains of homework and endless exams and tests. So **DON'T** be amazed that our children start school at three years old and **DON'T** be shocked to see tiny tots carrying bulging schoolbags almost the same size as themselves.

DO expect to be charmed by our children. They all look very sweet with their little round faces and happy expressions.

DON'T imagine that our city has always been today's glittering metropolis. It only started to really take off after China opened up in 1979. Before that it was a bit less energetic and much less crowded and built up.

DON'T be surprised that our city is really two societies - local Chinese and everyone else - and that we may behave differently according to which one we're operating in.

DON'T smoke in our public buildings or spit in public - it's against the law.

DON'T deface our SAR or Chinese flags - it's also against the law.

DO carry an official document of identity with you (a passport is fine) as the law requires it. **DON'T** be upset if you're asked to produce it by government officials and the police. They have the right to do so. Banks and shops will also ask for an official document of identity and it may be difficult to obtain certain services without one.

We're all generally very law abiding in Hong Kong and the crime rate is very low. So unless you're mixed up with Triads (Chinese gangs), shady business deals, or prostitution, or live in an overcrowded housing estate, **DON'T** be concerned about crime. The most that may happen is that you'll be cheated by a shopkeeper, or a taxi driver may short-change you or try to charge US dollars instead of Hong Kong dollars, but such things can happen anywhere. Our city is generally safe for visitors, but **DO** be sensible. Hang on to your handbags and wallets and **DON'T** leave your valuables lying around in public places.

DO be prepared for the air conditioning in our shops, cinemas, offices and restaurants. It's usually freezing cold. You might think it's wasteful but the heat saps one's energy and to function efficiently we have to keep cool at all times. So **DO** take a light jacket or sweater with you when shopping, at work or on an evening out. And **DON'T** be at all surprised to find office workers wearing polo-neck sweaters in the height of summer because of the freezing aircon.

During the summer months there is a 'drip' zone on pavements from leaking air-conditioners. **DO** be careful to avoid it like all the other pedestrians are doing or you'll end up with a very wet head.

If you're caught short, there are public toilets in certain locations such as shopping malls, but they may not be as clean or dry as you would wish. The same goes for small restaurants, or cafes. If you want to be sure, **DO** use the facilities in the large hotels and **DON'T** look for toilets in MTR stations - there aren't any! **DON'T** forget to tip the toilet attendants in smart restaurants and hotels and **DO** carry tissues with you, just in case.

DO take extra care where you eat and what you eat. Hepatitis is endemic in Hong Kong so it's usually safer to avoid shellfish which is a common source of infection, especially in the hot season, although there shouldn't be any problem if you're eating in the more up-market restaurants where hygiene should be good. **DON'T** worry about mosquitoes as they're generally not malarial.

DO be careful about sunbathing or being out in the sun for too long. Both the heat and sun can be relentless and damaging to your health. You'll notice that we prefer to stay in the shade ourselves. **DO** take bottles of water with you when you go outside the urban areas.

DO expect to be caught up in a world of the survival of the fittest and to have to speed up to keep up. So **DO** be alert for queue jumping. We residents have got it down to a fine art.

DON'T be offended if no-one offers a seat to you in a crowded train or on a bus. Sometimes you may just be lucky but generally seats are only given up for small children who might otherwise get squashed in the crowds.

And **DON'T** expect people walking two or three abreast down the street to give way to you. Normally, you'll have to squeeze past as best you can.

DON'T look disgruntled if our cleaners sweep the floor under your restaurant table while you're eating your meal or dust the telephone whilst you're in the middle of a call. **DO** just smile and lift your feet, or make your call again without complaint, because we've got to get our work done according to our strict routines whether you're in the way or not.

DON'T be surprised to find yourself in the noise capital of Asia. The decibel levels are unbelievable! **DON'T** be overwhelmed at the amount of talking that goes on - we're all very chatty (especially in our own language) and don't like silence. Even in hospitals, the noise and clatter is stupendous. And **DON'T** be fooled into thinking we're having an argument just because we're talking loudly at one another. No-one understands what you're saying if you just mumble in our language.

DON'T be confrontational or lose your temper or you risk losing face. For us, arguments are differences of opinion where we negotiate in order to come to an agreement. Generally patience and perseverance are likely to be more successful than shouting and displays of anger which just alienate people like us. But if there's no better way, some screaming and shouting will certainly get you attention!

DON'T beckon anybody over by using individual fingers. The polite way to beckon is with your palm downwards, waving all four fingers up and down together. And **DON'T** rub thumb and finger together to indicate money. It's very rude.

DO hand credit cards, calling cards, presents and anything else to us with two hands. The same goes for accepting things. We consider using only one hand to be very bad manners.

DO get used to the fact that Saturday mornings are Flag Days in our city. The flag sellers are usually school children and **DON'T** think you can avoid them because they pop up EVERYWHERE.

It's said that our city has the highest per capita consumption of cognac and Rolls Royce owners in the world. **DO** expect to drink toasts in cognac, and **DO** look out for the famous pink Rolls Royce in the Central District on Hong Kong Island. No, you haven't had too much cognac. The chauffeur garbed in pink is real!

Our city has a reputation for selling fake luxury goods but the government has been cracking down on such trade over the last few years. **DO** be careful about buying fakes, especially CDs and computer software. There are rumours that anyone caught POSSESSING a fake may be prosecuted in future.

Our city is run by civil servants. We do have a few political parties but they are still in their infancy and tend to be either pro-democracy, pro-China or pro-business and China. In the past we would have advised **DON'T** expect much political controversy or even political discussion in the newspapers, on the radio, or even at the personal level since Chris Patten's departure. But the economic slump, job losses and the anti-subversion law (see below) have been more recently galvanizing people into word and action.

Even so, we have always valued our right to protest in public whether it's in support of the Tiananmen student martyrs or the negative equity suffered by our property in the price slump. Street protests are often about livelihood issues, the state of the economy and what to do about the environment. But there have been

gatherings protesting about China-born relatives being given right of abode in Hong Kong, the government's powers of land purchase and compensation and, most recently, Article 23 of the Basic Law, the anti-subversion clause wherein fundamental freedoms under the concept of "One Country, Two Systems" are to be defined.

And a word about rubbish. Do use the colour-coded bins for bottles, paper and plastic waste. We're still not as environmentally-friendly as we should be at the moment - but we're working on it!

Hong Kong is a very convenient city. **DON'T** expect to have to go far to get anywhere or buy anything and **DON'T** expect too much bother in getting things done.

And finally:

Tipping

DON'T tip very much in Hong Kong. There is no 15 percent rule or anything like that. Taxi drivers don't expect very much - a maximum of HK$5 is enough. Credit card slips in restaurants will leave the bottom line for you to sign and add your own tip. Since there's a 10 percent service charge already, again, **DO** tip only a few (HK) dollars.

CHARACTER
TRAITS

You might think we're very like our fellow countrymen all over the world but we do have a few idiosyncrasies which make us very special. In some cases we're so unusual that you might think you've found yourself in the middle of a looking glass world.

Face

Governing our behaviour is the concept of face. This means that we try not to shame anyone or make them look ridiculous, and we try not to do anything that may cause us or our family to lose face, i.e., other people's respect (this is known in Cantonese as *mo min*). We try to avoid arguments or confrontation to preserve harmonious relations. So **DO** try not to be confrontational and **DO** recognise the good points of our argument before putting your own views forward. In short, **DO** 'give face' to us whenever you can.

Sometimes you may suspect we're being economical with the truth. We think of elaborate excuses to save face on both sides rather than just saying No. "Sorry I won't be free tomorrow night because my grandmother's dying in hospital and that's the last time I'll have a chance to see her" may just mean we have something better to do. And **DON'T** be surprised if next week it's our father's second sister we're worried about.

Fatalism

DON'T be surprised that we accept many events and injustices with an amazing equanimity. *Hai gam ge la* (That's how it is) and *Mo baan faat* (There's no other way) are our common responses to adverse situations. So **DON'T** be surprised at our ability to *hek foo* (eat bitterness) and to show amazing qualities of endurance even under the most difficult circumstances.

Family loyalty

Confucian philosophy has had a profound effect on our life, culture and behaviour. It governs the relationships and responsibilities between family (including relatives, in-laws, and very close friends), colleagues and associates, and strangers. To us, there are concentric circles of loyalty. Responsibility to our families comes first and we generally feel and show great respect for the older generation (this is called *haau sun* or 'filial piety'). We preserve our ancestral tablets in special clan halls whilst small ancestral altars can usually be found in most of our homes. Tradition has meant that we have been reluctant to help others and indeed in earlier times, if we did help a stranger, we might have been forced to take on responsibility for them - for their medical treatment, housing, food and general welfare. It may seem like selfishness but it is in fact a means of self-preservation in a harsh, hostile and competitive world.

Family loyalty is often translated to the workplace, and the nation, where our boss or national leader will act in a paternalistic way, being considered head of the family/nation and expected to protect his staff/people.

DON'T be surprised if your neighbours keep themselves to themselves and **DON'T** expect us to discuss our families in more than general terms. The Monday question "What did you do over the weekend?" isn't a Hong Kong question. On the other hand, because of these family networks, the Hong Kong grapevine must be the fastest in any of the world's big cities.

Guanxi (or gwaan hai to us Cantonese)

Chinese society is driven by personal relationships called *guanxi* in Mandarin Chinese, something like the 'old boys' network' or 'old school tie' network in other countries. This has good and bad points. It can be a wonderful lever in getting to know people, and in our progress up the career ladder. It can offer tremendous security for both us and our family members and a smoother path through life. It can also be very unfair - but then who expects life to be fair! And sometimes having continual obligations to others can be very burdensome.

DON'T stand in judgement on *guanxi*. It can be helpful to each and every one of us but like all forms of power it is open to abuse. Most of us use it wisely to do our best for our families and only a small minority tries to exploit it too much to their advantage.

So **DO** expect us to ask you to do favours for our friends or family and **DO** expect those favours to be returned in kind in the future. And **DO** be careful when talking about other people. Hong Kong is a very small place and all kinds of inter-relationships and *guanxi* exist.

Inscrutability

Some people say that Chinese are inscrutable. But in fact Chinese in general and we in Hong Kong in particular are human beings like everyone else and express our thoughts and emotions very publicly. Just like you, we laugh and cry and show our frustrations. Nevertheless, we may control our feelings in the presence of foreigners or our superiors, either in deference to them or to save face on both sides.

Amongst family, friends and fellow workers, we're pretty lively, far more expressive than the average Englishman, and more akin to Italians.

DON'T be surprised if a friendly conversation sounds like a heated quarrel.

DO be prepared for lots of loud voices and animated behaviour, especially facial expressions and hand gestures. Even visitors, when interacting with shop assistants, taxi drivers and hotel employees and despite not knowing the language, will be able to see how lively we are.

Superstition

We Hong Kong Chinese are profoundly superstitious. Numbers, colours and symbols all have an immeasurable influence over our lives. We've adopted some Western superstitions as well. Property developers for example, often avoid calling a floor the 13th so **DON'T** be surprised if a there's no 13 on the lift panel.

DON'T be surprised if we refuse to live in or buy property close to hospitals or graveyards for fear of ghosts. We avoid anything related to death at all costs.

DO expect a lack of interest in making wills or buying life insurance (insurance salesmen generally have a hard time in Hong Kong!).

DO remember that the number 4 is particularly unlucky, sounding as it does like the word for death (*sei* in Cantonese). Take a look - there is no number 4 booth in Hong Kong Jockey Club betting shops.

On the other hand, we consider the number 8 to be very lucky, as it rhymes with *faat*, the word for making money. So the seaweed, *faat choi*, is also considered lucky since in Chinese it resembles the words for becoming prosperous, as in the greeting *Gung hei faat choi* used at Chinese New Year.

DO remember the metaphors of colour: red is related to happy events and is the dominant colour at weddings and on other auspicious occasions such as Chinese New Year festivities; yellow was once the colour reserved for the emperor alone; white and black are the dominant colours at funerals and memorial services; green indicates a man has been cuckolded - 'wearing a green hat' is the local expression. The colours and designs on our opera masks denote whether the character wearing it is good or evil.

The Chinese word for a fish, *yue,* sounds the same as the word meaning abundance, so to us fish symbolise wealth. The Chinese word for chopsticks, *faai ji*, sounds the same as 'a son will arrive quickly' so a pair of chopsticks may be given to a newly-married couple as an auspicious present since we traditionally have a preference for boys over girls. If we have a son already and give birth to a daughter, a friend will comment *ho ji* meaning 'the character for good' which is a combination of the characters for 'son' and 'daughter'.

Whenever a project is started or completed, a ceremony will be held involving a priest and a roast suckling pig. This is very common in our movie industry where such rites have to be performed before filming begins to avoid any disasters. These rites also take place when the foundations of a building are laid and as part of the topping out ceremonies once things are completed.

DON'T be surprised at the number of fortune tellers in Hong Kong.

DO go to Kowloon's Temple Street on any evening to see all the different varieties of fortune-telling (palmistry, phrenology, birds, fortune sticks...). And **DO** check the various chapters on festivals, births, marriages and deaths to find out what the basic beliefs are on these occasions.

Meaning of life

Several traditional Chinese taboos, and their explanations as given by a fortune teller, were listed recently in the local press:

1. Breaking bowls during Lunar New Year: if your rice bowl is broken, you will starve for the rest of the year.
2. Pregnant women using scissors: their babies could be hyperactive.
3. Pregnant women eating prawns or crabs: their children will be rebellious.
4. Spilling water on your wedding day: the marriage will not last.
5. Giving children lucky names when they are small: they may use up their luck before they grow older. That is why so many rural Chinese children are given nicknames like 'little dog', 'little cow', and 'prawn head'.

Fung shui (or fung sui in Cantonese)

Fung shui, or geomancy, permeates every aspect of our lives in Hong Kong. Good *fung shui* (meaning 'wind and water') can bless a home or office with good luck and prosperity, whereas bad *fung shui* will bring misfortune to all who come into contact with it. It is difficult to get buyers or tenants for properties with bad *fung shui* and there have been many incidents in which we have objected to construction work or even to a tree being pulled down because of the effect on the *fung shui*. It is said that the Chief Executive, Mr Tung Chee-wa, declined to live in Government House because of its bad *fung shui*.

Fung shui is an ideal combination of the elements 'wind and water'. All of us know enough about it to make sure the layout of our homes and offices or the arrangement of our furniture won't cause bad luck. If bad luck befalls our family or business, we will call in the *fung shui lo* (the *fung shui* expert) to make suggestions as to what has to be done to improve the *fung shui*.

A Hong Kong *fung shui* master described in the local press how he uses his compass to determine if a location is good or bad, according to the mountains (buildings in the city) and the water (streets). He studies the site's relationship with other buildings, the shape of the building, the traffic flow, the location of the lifts, where the main door is sited and which way it opens. Then he looks at the office itself and determines where the conference room should be, where the manager's office should be, where to put the fax machine and how desks should be placed to avoid bad *chi* (energy).

Fung shui was certainly the reason why Ma On Shan villagers accused a property developer of letting a malevolent atmosphere permeate their village in 1998. By destroying a screen of 120 trees planted a few hundred years ago to protect all future generations of villagers from the 'killing force emanating from the north of Sai Kung', several catastrophes had befallen the village. A diabetic died within 24 hours of the travesty and an outbreak of strokes had mysteriously occurred. Determined to halt these calamities, a *fung shui lo* was called with the venerable gentleman proclaiming that the trees had prevented the three killing forces from hitting the village and moving the village god. The 'three killings' apparently meant livestock, humans and wealth in the village.

DO look out for: the *baat gwa* (small, eight-sided mirrors with decorative frames denoting the eight trigrams of the *Book of Changes*) which are put up in odd places to deflect bad luck; blocked off windows; oddly-arranged furniture; paper windmills in areas where the bad luck can be 'blown' away; or a new doorway in an unusual spot.

DO look out for graves and burial pots on hillsides where the *fung shui* is good. And **DO** have a look at the antennae on the Bank of China building which were considered daggers destined to bring bad times to Hong Kong.

Me first?

DO you find we lack consideration for others? We use our portable phones in cinemas, theatres, conferences, lecture theatres, hospitals, libraries and virtually everywhere. Our pagers go off all over the place. We bump into you in the street as if you weren't there and, without a word of apology; we close doors and lifts in your face. You can find yourself left holding a door open while we all stream in and out without a second glance at you.

We're not very good at waiting our turn and unsurprisingly we haven't always thought much of the famous British queue.

DON'T be amazed if we try to push in although nowadays quite a few of us are less tolerant of such behaviour.

DON'T expect us to be the first to step aside on the pavement or wait for you to precede us through the door. Life in Hong Kong is competitive, time is money, so **DON'T** be annoyed if we close the lift doors right in your face or hold the door open while we finish a phone call on our mobile.

DO be prepared for the bus to be driven off as you race to get on.

DON'T expect our cinema and theatre-goers to turn off their portable phones and pagers while the films are on. Telling friends where we are and what's happening on the screen is part of the fun of a night out.

DON'T presume we'll turn up before the start of a show. Many of us are bound to arrive late and will need to push past you.

DON'T expect your neighbours to conduct their lives quietly in deference to you but **DO** feel free to be just as noisy. We'll rarely complain.

You and us

Our society is very close-knit and, some would say, indifferent or even quite racist towards outsiders. It's quite true that we tend to feel that we from the Middle Kingdom are superior. As the story goes, when God made the world, Caucasians were underdone, Africans were overdone, but the Chinese were baked just right.

But **DON'T** be surprised to find we also have a hierarchy of discrimination amongst the many regions and nationalities of China itself. Beijingers are barbarians from the north; new arrivals from Guangdong province are often treated as *daai heung lei* (country bumpkins). However, Shanghainese are treated with a certain respect as we consider them to be very sophisticated and clever and even better than us at business.

DON'T be dismayed to find that however long you live in Hong Kong, it will be difficult to accept you as one of us unless you marry into a Chinese family, work in a very Chinese organisation, or speak our language with some fluency.

DO watch out for shopkeepers in tourist areas such as Tsim Sha Tsui or Causeway Bay charging you higher prices than necessary, and **DO** shop around. Taxi-drivers may tell you their meters are in US, not HK, dollars but **DON'T** fall for it.

And **DON'T** be hurt if we don't smile back at you if you're trying to be friendly. We're wary of strangers and will tend to think you're nuts.

Chinese medicine

Although you'll see Western style pharmacies everywhere, we still tend to be firm believers in Chinese medicine - and many of us still think carefully about what goes into our bodies. We drink concoctions and eat food which will have therapeutic effects and prevent and cure disease. The two opposite yet complementary forces of *yin* and *yang*, and the idea of disease as an imbalance of

the two, are
fundamental to
Chinese medicine.
We always talk
about food and
drink being *yit hei* (literally
'hot air') and *leung*
(cooling). So, if you feel
faint after drinking green tea it's because it's too *leung*, and you
shouldn't drink coffee when you have a cold because it's *yit hei*. We
use all sorts of herbs, roots and animal parts for health purposes.

DO expect many of us to have an
almost neurotic
concern with diet and
nutrition and **DON'T** be
intimidated by what you
find in your soup - it's
sure to be of proven
nutritional value.

DO try one of the
concoctions in a herbal tea
shop. Most of the drinks will be
really bitter, but if you prefer something sweet, you can have a nice
leung glass of sugarcane juice instead.

DON'T be surprised at the amount of Chinese tea taken with
our meals. It helps to wash down all the oil and fat used in
Cantonese cooking so **DO** have a few cups if you're over-
indulging.

Hanging out

One of our favourite pastimes is walking around the streets
window-shopping, which we call *haang gaai*. Since the majority of

our homes are small and not convenient for entertaining, *haang gaai* is an inexpensive way of having a good time with friends and family.

DON'T be surprised to find the streets bustling with groups of us ambling along enjoying themselves, especially on weekends.

Anarchists all

Despite adhering to traditional Confucian values and being generally very law abiding, there's a strong streak of anarchism in all of us. Historically, Guangdong Province (in which Hong Kong is located) has been a centre of rebellion against the central government and even today we don't quite understand the meaning of 'illegal' or 'prohibited'. Where rules can be broken they will be and that's one of the things that makes our society so dynamic, unexpected and interesting.

DO look out for cyclists pedalling the wrong way down a one-way street or crossing junctions against red lights.

DO be prepared for drivers making U-turns over double white lines or on blind corners and **DO** watch out for drivers jumping the lights.

And **DON'T** be amazed that we ran gambling syndicates during the 1998 World

Cup and the Euro 2000 Quarter Finals matches even though gambling is illegal in Hong Kong (except when run by the Jockey Club). But **DO** note that the authorities eventually gave in to the Jockey Club's complaints about loss of revenue because of Internet and illegal gambling. In July 2003 a gambling license was issued to the Jockey Club allowing them to receive bets on soccer games with the exception of local matches.

Keeping in touch

In busy Hong Kong, time means money. Keeping in constant touch with brokers, businesses, colleagues, friends and families is very important to everyone. Portable phones have made this so much easier and these days nearly one half of our population has a mobile phone (i.e., 60 percent of the population - just imagine!). The sound of phones (and pagers) can be heard everywhere. We walk around with hands (and phones) constantly pressed to ears, heads bowed, talking into space at the tops of our voices about

all kinds of personal matters. Because of this, our personal lives are constantly in the public domain, but we don't mind at all.

DON'T be shocked to hear the lady in front of you on the minibus calling up her broker or her friend in California on her portable phone.

DO expect phones to go off in cinemas and **DON'T** be surprised if the person sitting next to you rings up his mate two rows behind to discuss the film.

DON'T expect to shame us either with fierce glares or loud complaints into stopping our calls until they come to a natural end. It rarely works.

The group

The group is very important indeed to us, whether it be family, relatives, colleagues or friends. We find it difficult if not impossible to function if we're on our own. Going out in groups or holding group activities are favourite activities. Whatever we're doing - whether having lunch, going shopping, hiking in the New Territories, going on holiday, or even going to the washroom - we prefer to go with someone. Nowhere is this more obvious than at the airport. So when you arrive **DO** look out for the large groups of friends and relatives meeting and seeing off passengers.

DON'T be offended at our indifference to people outside the group. But once you're a member of a group, **DO** be prepared to be a member for life.

Fong bin

One of the reasons we're usually reluctant emigrants is the concept of *fong bin* (convenient). *Fong bin* means we don't have to walk far to get anywhere or buy anything. It means that things can get done without too much bother. It means minimal bureaucracy and not much interference in our personal affairs. In short, it means the Hong Kong way of life which we're all so used to and love so much.

DON'T be surprised to hear us complaining about having to go from Hong Kong Island to Kowloon (a 4-minute MTR ride) because it isn't *fong bin*.

DO expect us to take some kind of transport for even short distances; having to go on foot for more than a few yards isn't considered *fong bin*.

DON'T be surprised when emigrants return because things in the other country aren't *fong bin*.

A letter in the local press in 1999 from the Commissioner for Transport responding to a reader's suggestion that the government install pay-and-display machines in car parks, illustrates this typical Hong Kong dilemma:

> *'...each PDM governs a number of parking spaces. There is some public resistance to PDMs, owing to the walking distance between the parking space and the PDM and the queuing time that may be involved'.*

Despite this resistance, PDMs are creeping up on us in a few choice locations, encouraging our reluctant citizens to get in just that little bit of extra exercise from time to time.

Local manias

Hong Kong is a manic society - you name the mania, we've got it - and this is one of the things that makes Hong Kong buzz.

Gambling and speculating

Gambling is supposedly illegal in Hong Kong (except when organised by the Hong Kong Jockey Club) but we have a reputation as inveterate gamblers. In many ways this has been the driving force behind Hong Kong's spectacular growth since the early nineteen-eighties, with the opening up of China as the catalyst. We pour money into speculative ventures and risk all in the belief that the stock market will go on rising forever. Billions are spent on horseracing and the Mark 6 lottery.

DO take a look around any building site or in any small store and you're sure to find people gambling on *mahjong*, cards or dice. And millions were confiscated from illegal betting during the 1998 World Cup and Euro 2000 matches.

Coupon mania

One form of investment unique to Hong Kong is the coupon. Coupons can be bought in advance from cake shops and video/DVD rental stores. We hoard coupons for later use in the hope that their value will go up with inflation. One cake coupon is usually worth one dozen cakes, but video coupons may have a variety of values. Cake 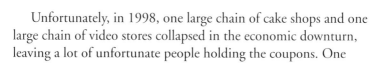 coupons especially are part of our culture and we distribute them to relatives, friends, guests and colleagues on auspicious occasions and particularly prior to weddings. Video coupons are a marketing ploy.

Unfortunately, in 1998, one large chain of cake shops and one large chain of video stores collapsed in the economic downturn, leaving a lot of unfortunate people holding the coupons. One woman had saved up 500 cake coupons and was distraught - her DESSERTS had DESERTED her. So be warned! **DO** be sure to use up any coupons as soon as possible.

Japanese popular culture mania

We're crazy over things Japanese. We especially like cute little icons such as Little Twin Stars and Hello Kitty and enjoy trips to Hello Kitty Land in Tokyo. Hello Kitty is a dear (or ultra-sickly - depending on your point of view) little white stuffed cat with a bow on its ear and currant-bun eyes which has captured the hearts of several generations of children. But Hello Kitty mania is not just a childhood fad.

DON'T be surprised that we adults wear Hello Kitty clothes, carry Hello Kitty backpacks, drive pink Hello Kitty cars, and use Hello Kitty credit cards. One of our legislators was even spotted writing in his Hello Kitty notebook during a debate.

Snoopy mania

McDonald's conducted a very successful marketing campaign, offering one different plastic Snoopy out of a collection of 28 each day for one month for every Big Mac meal purchased. What began as a rather sluggish campaign reached fever pitch as the investment value of Snoopy dolls suddenly soared. Rubbish bins at every outlet were filled with unwrapped burger meals while the dolls were hoarded or traded. Two major public holidays saw queues of parents at McDonald's outlets waiting patiently to collect the latest Snoopy for their offspring. At the same time, the complete set could have been purchased off the shelf in Thailand and other South-East Asian countries without any hassle! A few months later, history repeated itself with the launching of a serial Hello Kitty toy, again by McDonald's.

It was reported at the time that a woman collapsed while queuing for McDonald's most sought-after toy - Hong Kong Snoopy - and refused medical attention for fear of losing her place; that a scuffle and several injuries resulted as tens of thousands of people swamped outlets to buy a Snoopy toy dressed as a fisherman; and that long queues and high humidity frayed the tempers of many, including a young man and an older woman, who tussled outside an outlet in Mongkok.

Sense of humour

We like having fun and especially appreciate Charlie Chaplin and his banana-skin slapstick-style humour. We don't understand sarcasm but the Chinese language lends itself well to word play and satire.

DON'T be aghast if we stand and laugh when someone falls over and, unless you're a fluent Chinese speaker, **DON'T** ever expect to understand the brilliant play on words, double entendre, and humorous misunderstandings that our monosyllabic language lets us make.

The *mou lei tau* or 'nonsense' style of humour is a favourite type of comedy wherein the actors fool around and act idiotically to roars of laughter from the audience.

The language is also full of imagery and metaphor. So 'dried beef' is a parking ticket, 'feeding the tiger' is putting money in the parking meter, and 'chasing the dragon' is taking drugs.

FOOD AND
DINING

Hong Kong is the food capital of China and has thousands of restaurants, small cafes, noodle shops and street stalls. Pre-Revolution chefs fled south in 1949 and set up business in Hong Kong. The saying goes: Be born in Suzhou (which has China's most beautiful women), Live in Hangzhou (China's most beautiful city), Eat in Hong Kong (this used to be Eat in Guangzhou before 1949), Die in Liuzhou (where the best wood for coffins can be found).

Food is very important to us on account of the frequent wars, famines and other disasters to which we've been subjected during our turbulent history. Instead of saying 'hello' when we greet people, we often say *Sik faan mei a?* (Have you eaten yet?). We spend much of our time eating and enjoy taking people out to restaurants rather than entertaining them in our tiny homes.

For breakfast, we may eat rice porridge with *yau ja gwai* ('oil-fried foreigner' dough sticks) at a small food stall or have several

plates of snacks in a restaurant while meeting friends or family, showing off our birds, or reading the newspaper. The snacks range from spring rolls to chicken feet and are called *dim sum* ('little bits of heart'). We may have more *dim sum* at lunchtime, or just a *faan haap* (a box of rice, meat and vegetables) in the office or workplace. In the evening we'll have rice, soup, and meat and vegetable dishes at home with all the family, or go to a restaurant to entertain or relax. Very few of us go without three proper meals a day if we can help it.

There's a vast body of popular lore relating to health and diet in our cuisine. We consider various foods to be directly related to promoting health and longevity. Most of us pay great attention to what we eat to prevent disturbing our constitutions which can be either 'hot' or 'cold'. Illness is actually considered a constitutional imbalance so an appropriate food should be taken to restore that balance.

As in Chinese medicine, certain foods are considered *yit hei* (heating to the body) and others, *leung* (cooling), and there are prescribed conditions for taking one or the other. 'Cold' people can eat spicy food, but people with a cold should avoid coffee at all costs. And by tradition certain foods have to be served at particular festivals. On a festival such as *Dung Jit* (Winter Solstice), for example, chicken has to be served.

General reminders:

DO remember that Chinese meals are a communal affair so dishes are normally shared by everyone.

If you're given a hot towel to refresh your hands and face, **DON'T** blow your nose into it and **DON'T** use it for a general body wash.

DO order a rice and meat dish with a plate of vegetables for a cheap and nutritious meal.

DON'T worry about spilling anything onto tablecloths. It's expected. Fresh cloths are usually laid for all new diners.

DON'T feel embarrassed about pointing to what somebody else is eating if you can't read the menu.

DO use chopsticks if you can although a Chinese spoon is perfectly acceptable if it's too difficult for you. In larger restaurants, knives and forks may be provided for non-Asians as a matter of course. If you're left-handed, **DO** try to use your right hand for chopsticks - otherwise you may get entangled with your neighbour at meals as Chinese uniformly are brought up to use their right hands for eating.

DO lift your bowl up to your mouth and shovel the food in with your chopsticks. We all do it and it's the best way to enjoy your meal.

DO be careful not to mistake the finger bowls for drinking water.

DO slurp your soup or noodles just like we locals do.

DON'T be surprised if your companions burp their approval at the end of the meal. It's expected as a sign of enjoyment and satisfaction.

DO take your time when eating. You can usually spend a whole morning over just a few *dim sum* without any pressure to leave unless there are crowds of people waiting for a table.

DON'T expect to be able to pay by credit card except in the

larger restaurants. **DO** carry sufficient cash to pay for snacks and small meals.

DO remember: hepatitis is endemic in Asia and is typically carried by shellfish so **DO** choose your eating place carefully, especially in summer when nasty diseases are particularly prevalent.

Yes, we know it's complicated but **DON'T** be put off. The food can be spectacular and it's really great fun (and we all talk with our mouths full)!

Dai pai dong (Food stalls)

You can find food stalls in the streets all over Hong Kong, but they're not one hundred per cent hygienic although the food's usually very good. The owner of Hong Kong's world-famous Yung Kee Restaurant started off with just his own food stall. In some areas, you can order dishes from different stalls, pay for each one separately, then sit at any table you like and wait for the food to be delivered to you.

DO expect to sit on wobbly stools at wobbly tables by the roadside or right in the street itself.

DO eat at a stall which looks busy and popular - the food should be very good.

DON'T be shocked if fellow-diners spit their meat and fish bones onto the table. **DO** it too if you feel like it.

DO expect to have to pay in cash.

DO remember that no tips or service charge are required.

Small cafes/noodle shops

These will be more comfortable than a *dai pai dong* and generally serve noodle or rice dishes. The ones in working class areas will be very basic and cramped but the food will usually be good and cheap. In recent years, there has been a trend towards more up-market small eateries, many of them furnished and decorated in traditional Chinese style. Their menus are often selected for particular nutritional value

DON'T expect the menu to be in any language except Chinese, although you may just be lucky.

DO feel free to point at what others are eating to indicate what you would like.

DO expect to be served quickly and to leave quickly once you've had your meal.

DON'T expect service to be very courteous though if you smile a lot the waiters will probably smile back.

DO pay your bill in cash at the till at the door.

DO put your small change from the bill in the saucer near the till if you're pleased with the service and/or food.

Restaurants

Hong Kong restaurants are usually large and very noisy. On Sunday mornings they are often filled to capacity with entire families for whom going for *yam cha* (drinking tea, i.e., *dim sum*) is the favourite Sunday outing. In traditional restaurants, the *dim sum* will be served from trolleys which are wheeled amongst the tables for you to choose from. You'll be given a card divided into various price categories and a chop (i.e., stamp) will be made under the relevant category for each dish you take. At the end of the meal, the waiter will take the card and you'll be charged according to the number of chops in each category. In some restaurants, the baskets and dishes are piled up on the table as you finish them and the bill is calculated from the number

and size of the different baskets and dishes. Hotel restaurants also serve *dim sum*, but the variety will be limited, you'll have to order them first and they'll be delivered direct to your table.

DO stop the trolley and ask for a dish you like.

DO remember that *yam cha* should be leisurely and dishes will continuously appear, so there's no need to rush into taking as many as you can all at once and loading them onto your table.

DO ask the opinion of any guests you invite about what kinds of dishes they would like to eat.

DO order several plates of a dish if you have a large gathering of friends. There should usually be one item on the dish for each person at the table. If there isn't, **DO** order two or three of the same dish.

DO push the dishes closer to your guests to invite them to eat first, or offer them an item with your chopsticks before tucking in yourself.

DON'T eat more than your share unless it's obvious some pieces of food will be left over.

DON'T finish off a dish without first inviting your companions to eat the remaining items.

DO order dishes of noodles or vegetables to accompany your *dim sum* meal.

Evening meals in restaurants are usually more formal. A menu will be offered to you and the waiter will suggest which of the dishes are particularly good that day. In less elegant restaurants, the menu may be only in Chinese, but the waiters can often dig out a page with quaint English translations from somewhere.

Inviting guests

As we've said, eating in a Chinese restaurant is usually a leisurely affair lasting several hours. You'll generally be allowed to finish your meal in your own time. If you're seated at a large table, the dishes will be placed on a lazy susan (a turntable device in the middle of the table) which you or your guests can swivel around to get at the dish you want.

DO expect to be given a choice of tea to drink and **DO** realise it will be part of the cover charge. To be on the safe side, **DO** order *heung pin* (jasmine) which is a pleasant, light and refreshing tea.

DO expect to be given snacks, such as peanuts or pickled vegetables, in larger restaurants. These will also be charged to your bill.

DO ask the exact price for the whole order of any seafood. The price quoted in the menu may only be per *tael* (Chinese ounces), not for the exact item or quantity.

DO check whether bowls of rice have to be ordered separately from the main dishes as they may not be automatically provided without your asking for them.

DO help your guests to food, throughout the meal, before helping yourself.

DO swivel the lazy Susan around (slowly to avoid accidents!) to encourage your guests to try other dishes.

DO use the long 'public' chopsticks to serve others, or use your own turned upside down.

DO ask your guests' advice on what to order to ensure they enjoy the food too.

DO share everything and **DON'T** hog certain dishes yourself.

DON'T turn a fish over (or you'll 'overturn the boat', i.e., some misfortune will befall you). **DO** dig amongst the bones for the bits underneath.

DON'T eat the last piece of food on a dish (or you'll 'remain unmarried forever').

DO expect a service charge to be automatically included in the bill.

DO add an additional tip on your credit card docket or leave some small change on the platter when retrieving your receipt.

Invited by others

We tend to meet friends and family and do our entertaining in restaurants. So if you're invited out by others for a formal meal:

DO expect your hosts to settle the bill.

DON'T argue with your hosts about the bill or they'll lose face.

DO wait to be seated by the host.

DON'T order any food or drinks yourself. **DO** wait to be asked.

DON'T start eating until your hosts take up their chopsticks and invite you to tuck in or help you to food.

DO eat sparingly from each dish as many more dishes will appear in due course.

DON'T stuff yourself full from any one dish or you'll be unable to survive until the end of the meal.

DO take the piece of food nearest to you and **DON'T** reach right across the table for something you desperately want.

Someone will pass the dish over or help you to it eventually.

DON'T be surprised if the seat facing the door is reserved for the main guest (which may be you). This is our way of showing respect (and of keeping you safe in days gone by - no treacherous back-stabbing by your enemy!).

DON'T finish everything in your bowl or on your plate or your host will lose face for providing insufficient food.

DO tap the table three times with your knuckles when the tea is poured to say 'thank you' (symbolic of how we would *kow-tow* three times to the emperor in bygone days).

DON'T be alarmed when everyone disperses quickly at the end of the meal. It's quite normal.

Apart from Chinese restaurants, there is a large variety of international ones so **DO** try them out. Japanese, Korean and Indian restaurants are very popular. The Hong Kong Tourism Board booklet, and *bc Magazine* and *HK Magazine* which are available free from many hotels, bookshops and restaurants, list a variety of restaurants. But if you're at a loss, **DO** go to one of the international hotels which serve magnificent buffet lunches and suppers or just simple coffee shop food in elegant surroundings.

If it's sandwiches, boxes of sushi, salads and fruit, cakes and doughnuts you want, **DO** go to hotel and other cake shops and neighbourhood stores. And there's always the supermarket, the small store, or the street hawker for cheap drinks, fruit and chocolate. In all, food is so readily available, it's really difficult to go hungry in Hong Kong.

Finally - **DO** try our egg tarts - they're out of this world!

SHOPPING

Hong Kong has long enjoyed a reputation as a shopper's paradise. Tourists used to come here for bargain price cameras, videorecorders, calculators, cheap clothes and oriental nick nacks. More recently they've come for fake designer goods, computer software, CDs and other electronic products. They've wandered round the back streets and alleys and poked into tiny, crowded little shops to see what they can find at bargain prices. However, the nineteen-eighties economic boom, especially soaring property prices, and widespread urban renewal projects, has meant the end of many of the quaint little shops. And China's entry onto the world market has seen oriental curios available in almost every corner of the globe, not only in Chinatown areas, but also in upmarket department stores. Designer boutiques have still been able to entice tourists from wealthier countries such as Japan but the recession back home has seen the exodus of many local Japanese businesses and the many tour groups reduced to a trickle.

Shopping in the early nineties moved from our polluted but colourful streets into ubiquitous shopping malls, all conveniently linked to Mass Transit Railway stations, where eating, window-shopping and cinema-going in comfort under one air-conditioned roof is now a local pastime. But these days we are increasingly making day trips across the border to Shenzhen where food, clothing, leisure goods, and other daily necessities are very much cheaper.

The major shopping areas are Central, Causeway Bay, and Taikooshing on Hong Kong Island, Tsimshatsui and Mongkok in Kowloon, and Shatin in the New Territories. The majority of the large Japanese department stores closed down during the economic downturn, 1997-98, but most international clothing chains usually have outlets in all these areas. Central District, with its major department stores and designer boutiques, is still the area for elegant clothing. Local fashion chains sell casual wear at cheaper prices. Tailors still do good business but are now acting increasingly as middlemen between the customer and workers over the China border in Shenzhen where cheap labour means very reasonable prices.

Designer seconds can be found in factory outlets, in Granville

Road in Tsimshatsui, or at Stanley Market. A booklet listing factory outlets is on sale in local bookshops. Other cheap clothing and accessories can be found at markets in Temple Street and Women's Street, both in Kowloon, and Stanley Market on Hong Kong Island.

DO check the Hong Kong Tourism Board booklet available on arrival at the airport for outlets for Chinese arts and crafts, designer orientalia and any other items you wish to buy.

If you're looking for pirated CDs and other software, **DON'T**. The Hong Kong Government has regular blitzes on illegal software outlets and it's now increasingly difficult to find shops willing to take the risk.

DO go to the well known shopping malls, such as Times Square and Pacific Place on Hong Kong Island, and Ocean Centre, Ocean Terminal, and Festival Walk in Kowloon, if you want to shop in air-conditioned comfort.

DON'T expect department stores and many boutiques and smaller shops to open until the latter part of the morning but **DO** remember they tend to close quite late in the evening (except in Central).

DON'T be put off if the service in shops and taxis isn't particularly polite or attentive. The Hong Kong Tourism Board is trying hard to improve Hong Kong's image in this respect but there's still a long way to go. But when our service is good, you can expect it to be really excellent, particularly in hotels which usually offer first class customer care.

DO visit the stores when they have sales. The bargains and range of goods are much more extensive than other cities in the region.

DON'T get mad if people don't queue up and **DO** expect our shopkeepers to serve several people at once. Speed and efficiency is part of what Hong Kong's all about.

DO expect some pushing and shoving in the busy areas. **DON'T** forget there are almost 7 million people crammed into this crowded city of ours, so it's not really surprising.

DON'T try to bargain in department stores, shopping malls, and chain stores - goods are almost always sold at fixed prices in these places - but **DO** bargain in smaller shops and street markets. If you're dissatisfied, **DO** check nearby shops and stalls for cheaper prices.

DO expect a hierarchy of prices to be charged in street markets and small shops: if you're a local Chinese, you'll be given the cheapest price; the next price up is for Chinese from other parts of China; the next for overseas Chinese/Cantonese - speaking foreigners; and the highest is for non-Cantonese - speaking foreigners.

DON'T feel elephantine if large clothing sizes are difficult to find. Local people are generally petite and the average women's sizes are 4-6 in clothing and 2 in shoes. The average men's sizes are small-medium. And **DO** make sure that what you're buying is clean and properly finished, however cheap it is.

DO make sure you go to a tailor with a good reputation and **DO** allow enough time for alterations. Although our tailors are famous for getting clothes made with incredible speed, if alterations need to be done there may not be time before you're off to the airport.

Before you buy, **DO** make sure you know the difference between genuine 'jade' and other precious items sold by hawkers. There are plenty of booklets on the subject so **DON'T** get caught out.

DO be careful when buying camera and video equipment. Some retailers substitute inferior or used products after the sale has been made, or pretend that the model you want has just sold out, then insist you buy a more expensive one after you've paid up front.

DON'T sign your credit card docket or hand over any money until the actual product you want to buy is put on the counter in front of you.

DON'T be caught out and **DO** go to a respectable retailer even if it's more expensive than elsewhere.

DO ask for an international guarantee, and **DO** check that the user guide is in a language you can read.

DON'T smoke in shopping malls. From mid-1998 it's been against the law to do so.

Street Markets

Hong Kong is famous for its lively and colourful street markets where imitation designer clothes and accessories can be picked up quite cheaply.

Temple Street

DON'T miss a visit to Temple Street which is one of our most popular street markets. It's particularly lively and interesting in the evening when all the fortune tellers ply their trade and amateur singers perform.

DO look around carefully before you buy. There are hundreds of stalls selling the same goods but not all at the same price.

DON'T expect imitation goods to be displayed. You'll be shown photos of them and the items you choose will be fetched surreptitiously from elsewhere after you agree to buy.

DO expect to bargain a little but if you take it too far the shopkeeper will consider it a waste of time and serve somebody else.

DO have your fortune told or stand and watch while others do.

DO find time to listen to the street performers. The Chinese instruments are remarkable and sometimes the performers dress up in traditional costume.

DO remember that Temple Street has a reputation for gangsters, prostitutes, wide boys and other colourful characters although nowadays it's a pretty safe place to wander around.

Fa Yuen Street

DO venture along to the bustling precincts of Kowloon's Prince Edward Road West and mingle with the dense crowds of shoppers buying clothing in Fa Yuen Street and tropical flowers in the adjacent Flower Market. And **DO** include a visit to the Bird Garden nearby where exotic birds and beautifully crafted cages are for sale, and where owners take their birds to socialise. The whole of this area is full of local life.

Cat Street

Shopping for antiques has been traditionally associated with Upper Lascar Row, known as 'Cat Street' although there are clusters of both cheap and upmarket antique shops in the whole of that Hong Kong Island Hollywood Road area. Most fascinating are the tinier shops bursting with all kinds of bric-a-brac where you might just find something valuable amongst all the dusty items.

DON'T hesitate to bargain. Shop owners spring to life at some energetic give and take and really enjoy it.

DO check what you're buying very carefully. China tries to control what's exported and Hong Kong shops are more likely to sell replicas or fakes than the genuine article, particularly if the item is supposed to be 'ancient'. Fake paintings and objets d'art abound.

DO go to an upmarket retailer if you want genuine antiques. A certificate of authenticity will be supplied and the sales people should be knowledgeable about the item.

Stanley Market

DO take a trip out to Stanley, on the south side of Hong Kong Island, if you have the time. The original Stanley market consisted of a couple of streets filled with rather shabby shops and stalls selling fruit and vegetables, cheap clothing (some of it designer seconds) and oriental bric-a-brac. Some years ago it was given a facelift but the basic character was left intact and it still remains extremely popular with visitors.

Wet markets

Some fascinating hours can be spent in the open food markets as well. Although supermarkets are everywhere, we still go to these 'wet' markets several times a day to buy our food as it has to be really fresh for Chinese home cooking.

Wet markets were originally areas of the city where individual and often unlicensed hawkers congregated to sell their products from mobile carts or laid out on plastic sheets or newspapers by the roadside. Difficult to control and plagued by Triad rackets, the

areas have been mostly cleared and the hawkers relocated to air-conditioned and supposedly more hygienic indoor markets where licenses can be properly regulated.

Wet markets sell fresh foods and the whole place is literally 'wet'. Vegetables are dunked in buckets of water before being displayed, fresh fish are laid on glistening wet slabs or scooped out of huge tanks dripping wet, and floors are frequently hosed down for general hygiene. Wet markets can be found in all the working class districts and housing estates. Items will be weighed either in pounds on Western scales, or in *catties* or *taels* - equivalent to half a kilogram and one sixteenth of a kilogram respectively - on Chinese-style hand scales. Close by there will be stores selling dry provisions such as rice, dried beancurd, peanuts, spices, soya sauce, rice wine, etc.

DO be careful where you walk - the floors can be very wet and slippery and in places covered with bits of vegetables and other debris.

DO look out for the live animals - tanks of fish and cages of fowl, frogs, turtles, hairy crabs, and rice birds - and **DON'T** be horrified to see them killed and cut up for customers before your very eyes.

DO take a look at the open air butcher stalls where customers can select any cut they want, have the fat removed (even the tiniest bits), and get the meat chopped up or minced within a few seconds of buying it.

DO stop at the fresh fish stalls where the fishmonger will trim

and gut the fish for you with amazing speed and dexterity.

DON'T hesitate to bargain to get a better price.

DO pick through fruit to select the pieces you want. It's expected by most hawkers.

DON'T be surprised if what you buy is weighed on Chinese-style hand balances which you can't understand. Only the hawker or shopkeeper will know if you're getting a fair deal!

DON'T MISS Hollywood Road and the old Taipingshan Chinese quarter

DO find time to wander around the narrow winding streets of this old Chinese quarter on Hong Kong Island and **DO** purchase the guide to this area produced by the Hong Kong Tourism Board (*Central and Western District Heritage Trail and Walking Tour*).

DO enjoy a ride up or down the Central to Mid-Levels escalator to get a preview of some of the places of interest in the area and **DO** especially look out for the following:

Curio shops

DO rummage through these amazing Aladdin's caves of items at bargain prices: yellowing photos of old Hong Kong; dusty Chinese pottery and figurines; trays of jade pieces and other bric-a-brac; porcelain-lidded boxes trimmed with silver; chopstick holders; abacuses, packets of 'ancient' Chinese coins; cane-handle teapots; replicas of old posters of demure cheongsamed young ladies; carved cigarette holders; bead necklaces of all types of stones and colours; geomancer compasses; old China Motor Bus tickets; copies of Mao's 'Little red book', plus assorted Mao badges and other Cultural Revolution memorabilia; old vaccination certificates, vacuum cleaner guarantees and cinema tickets; ageing soft drink cans.

Paper shops

These shops provide all manner of items for use at Chinese festivals, religious ceremonies, marriages and funerals. Incense sticks, candles, bundles of 'hell' bank notes, cardboard dollars covered with foil, and colourful woodblock prints of deities, one of the most popular being Kuan Ti, the God of war. Such pictures are placed in strategic positions in our homes and temples to ward off evil spirits. These shops are where the paper models, such as houses, cars, television sets, for burning at funerals are made. The models can usually be seen hanging at the entrance or lying around in the dark recesses of the shop so **DO** step inside to have a look.

Lantern shops

DO stop and wonder at the shops selling lanterns at the time of the Moon Festival on the 15th day of the 8th month of the lunar calendar.

DON'T forget to take your camera to shoot the magnificent eye-catching displays of paper lanterns of almost every shape and size hanging from the shop doorways: bright red horses and butterflies scintillating with sequins, round smiling suns, gilded carp, and traditional red-tasselled Chinese lanterns.

Chinese provision shops

DO potter inside the Chinese provision shops which sell anything from bits of ginger and garlic to dried salt fish, fungus, mushrooms, rice, nuts of every variety, spices, soya sauce, canned luncheon meat, evaporated milk and packets of cigarettes.

Fruit and vegetable stalls

DO admire the displays on the lean-to street stalls with their neatly stacked piles of local vegetables and exotic fruits - mangoes, lychees, longans, papayas, pomelos, carambolas, durians, jackfruits - together with mounds of oranges, apples and bananas.

DO be adventurous and try out the fruits you've never seen before. What about a piece of durian? It may smell dreadful but the flesh is sublime (or so they say!).

Chop and seal stalls

Chops and seals are still widely used in Hong Kong and carving them with artistic Chinese characters requires special skills.

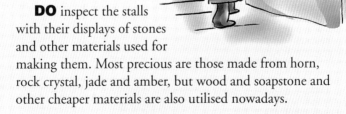

DO inspect the stalls with their displays of stones and other materials used for making them. Most precious are those made from horn, rock crystal, jade and amber, but wood and soapstone and other cheaper materials are also utilised nowadays.

DO ask the shopkeeper to make a seal for you and to give advice on a suitable stone and Chinese name.

Chinese medicine shops

Chinese medicine shops offer the visitor one of the most exotic and fascinating views of the magical orient.

DO venture inside to inspect the displays of ginseng, deer antlers, bull's penises, dried seahorses, insects, roots, leaves, seeds, berries and other exotic items.

DO watch what happens when a customer presents a prescription - the opening of one of the hundreds of drawers lining the interior walls; the weighing of the items on a Chinese-style scales; the trimming of large pieces with a huge sharp guillotine; and the expert division of mixtures of items into separate dosages. Once home, most of the products are boiled into concoctions and you may wonder what they're supposed to do. The answers would take more space than we have paper for, but rest assured that modern science confirms that the basis of much traditional Chinese medicine is sound and that many of these therapies really do work.

One of the most famous and busiest shops is Eu Yan Sang in Queen's Road Central which has a magnificent brass statue of a horse in the entrance. **DO** take a look. Here's

your chance to buy the spices and herbs for the steamed chicken soup you've always wanted to make and the shopkeeper will be happy to advise on the mix that's just right for you.

ENTERTAINMENT
AND THE MEDIA

We Chinese know how to enjoy ourselves. Hong Kong never seems to sleep and its citizens are always on the move. They tumble out of nightclubs, bars and discos in the wee hours causing people-jams. Traffic can be slow and heavy at 2 a.m. and even shops stay open to midnight or later in Tsim Sha Tsui and Wanchai. All this is possible because most of us want to get out of our small and crowded family flats to meet friends. We have a natural sense of togetherness and pleasure and the young have disposable incomes. Best of all, the laws of Hong Kong are amenable to late night carousing.

Weekends are when everything happens but **DON'T** be misled into thinking that workday evenings are dull affairs. Whatever you want to do is catered for in Hong Kong every day of the week.

DO check all the entertainment guides available in the daily newspapers and in free magazines like the monthly *bc Magazine* and weekly *HK magazine*. They list most things that are happening in Hong Kong.

DO go to or phone TICKETEK Cinemas - the city council's computerised ticket outlets - for most tickets to do with major events.

Even though others do it, please **DON'T** use your mobile phones and pagers in theatres and cinemas. (Yes - a cry in the dark - an earnest plea from the heart!).

Cinemas

Hong Kong is to Chinese cinema what Bombay is to Indian and Hollywood to the world. During the seventies and eighties, our film industry flourished and prospered with movie after movie going into production even before scripts were ready, and shooting being completed in only a few weeks. We especially used to love kung fu and gangster films, or a mixture of both. We were also

good at making ghost stories and costume dramas. These would often contain spectacular choreography, acrobatics, and people flying through the air with extravagant costumes and hairdos.

In recent years the film industry appeared to be on its last legs. Famous local talent such as John Woo and Jacky Chan, have been doing most of their work in Hollywood and audiences have been shrinking as more and more cinemas have preferred to show foreign films. Hollywood blockbusters have been wowing the crowds and films have been available on pirated DVDs almost before they come out of the developing tank. However, the lastest news is that this trend has started to reverse as audiences become fed up with formulaic Hollywood fodder. Local and Mainland film-makers once again are preferring more innovative projects.

DON'T bother to buy any pirated VCDs. The image on these disks is usually obscured by the large person sitting in front of the counterfeiter's videorecorder in the local cinema! (Incidentally, **DO** note the ushers in certain cinemas patrolling along the aisles during the show to stop this happening!).

DO catch a local movie if one is being shown. The fact that you don't speak the language will barely detract from your enjoyment of the film and the strange English of the subtitles will be an experience in itself.

All seats are bookable so **DO** buy tickets for a popular film well in advamce or you'll find yourself siting right up near the screen, cross-eyed and ears blasted by the Dolby sound. Hong Kong shows Hollywood films quite quickly, although art-house films are more difficult to find. True to form, Hong Kong's liberal disposition means that mainstream and independent films censored everywhere else in Asia, are often shown unmutilated by their distributors. If they are cut, it's because the distributor wants to fit them into a specific schedule (like a three-hour film into a two-hour time slot) and this can lead to some horrendous editing. Most shows are bookable in advance and the cinemas are generally clean although not necessarily comfortable.

DON'T expect luxury in the older cinemas.

DON'T expect people to stand up for you to pass by when you're trying to get to your seat.

DON'T smoke in any cinema. It's against the law.

DON'T expect to peacefully watch the film credits roll at the end. Everyone will already be up and heading for the exits, and the cleaners will be sweeping up the popcorn from around your feet.

DON'T canoodle in the cinema seats. It's generally just not done. (Come to think of it, where is it done in Hong Kong exactly?).

DON'T bother to complain if someone in front of you is:
- Using a mobile phone
- Smoking
- Gossiping

It's unlikely to do any good in the long run even though it may put a stop to it for a short while.

DO realise that Hong Kong has a great film tradition and going to the cinema is very popular here.

DO relax...you get the latest films quickly and the cinema chains are quite good.

DO go to the specialist cinemas if you're interested in art house films, or visit during the Hong Kong International Film Festival which takes place around Easter every year.

DO note that more challenging western and art house films will have a very short run.

DO remember that sometimes cinemas have a half price ticket day (currently Tuesday)...but **DO** book early - and on the same day.

Western drama and classical music

DO check for the Hong Kong Arts Festival - around January and February every year. It's the high point of the cultural calendar with lots of good things happening in quick succession. But there are always concerts and events throughout the year using local and visiting talent.

DO check the local papers and 'what's on' magazines or ask your hotel concierge.

Chinese classical music

DO go to a concert given by the Hong Kong Chinese Orchestra for a flavour of the richness of the Chinese musical tradition.

DO go to Temple Street in the evening to listen to impromptu performances of Cantonese opera.

Rock and pop

Western rock is available live in pubs and clubs and there are very occasional visits by big Western stars. However, **DO** realise western rock is largely ignored by the Hong Kong kids who regard the local, mostly clean cut Canto-pop stars like Aaron Kwok and Anita Mui as gods and goddesses.

Aside from the Coliseum in Kowloon (a huge basketball stadium affair), there are no big rock venues. The Hong Kong stadium was built for such events, but the first two concerts brought such ire and fire down from heaven (i.e., from the residents of the luxury apartments nearby), that the former Urban Council which ran it chickened out and wouldn't allow anyone there any more.

DO believe this because it's absolutely true! A concert at the stadium was scheduled for Elton John as part of the handover celebrations in mid-1997. After the former Council imposed anti-noise restrictions on Elton, including the issuance to all concert goers of head-phones for directly wired music, and gloves - yes gloves - to keep the noise of applause down, Elton turned down the chance of such a uniquely organised musical event.

Gambling

It's so endemic, we've devoted a whole paragraph to it in the chapter on Character Traits.

DO go to Macao if you want a casino. There are no legal ones in Hong Kong although there has been recent talk of introducing some to compete with Macao for tourists.

DON'T try and gamble your money away by

playing *mahjong*, even with friendly locals. You'll be left for dead!

DO bet only at the (now no longer 'Royal') Hong Kong Jockey Club outlets, either on the Races, the local lottery, the Mark Six or non-local soccer games. It's illegal to bet any other way.

DO go to the races at Happy Valley or Shatin. They're clean and safer on the wallet. It's also a spectacular occasion, with a huge TV screen to see what's happening if you haven't brought your binoculars. You can eat or drink there too, so **DO** buy your food before you bet!

DO get a guide to betting from the Hong Kong Jockey Club stewards at the race courses and in the betting shops dotted around Hong Kong. They'll also help you to mark the betting cards in the right way.

DON'T be embarrassed that everyone else seems to know what to do. We are serious gamblers, and have got the whole thing down to a fine art. The 'profits' from Jockey Club betting have financed good works and public buildings all over Hong Kong. So...

DON'T be surprised if the old man in torn singlet and oily shorts ahead of you in the betting queue lays down thousands of Hong Kong dollars in cash for a bet. This is quite normal in Hong Kong.

Television

DO watch local TV. There are four terrestrial channels:

- HOME   Chinese
- JADE   Chinese
- WORLD   English, with *putonghua*, Japanese and
          Korean hours.
- PEARL   English with ditto.

The two companies that run these four channels are bound by law to provide English services. This they find increasingly irksome and expensive.

DON'T be surprised to see the English channels full of hours of boring (and cheap) racing coverage - unless you like racing of course - but it's better to see it live at Happy Valley or Shatin (forget Macao).

But...where else in the world would you find TWO reasonably decent TV channels speaking in the area's second language? They do show good feature films (with lots of adverts), sometimes well before anyone else on the globe gets them terrestrially.

DO check the daily newspaper for a programming guide. The companies change their schedules without much notice and are fiercely competitive with one another. If one shows a Stallone film, the other will change its programme to show another with the same star. Quality programmes also appear at the strangest times. The TV executives must buy in bulk, because sometimes they put on a superb programme which they obviously do not rate (or have not seen) at 11.00 a.m. on a Saturday morning.

DON'T watch the trailers for the upcoming films on TV. Annoyingly, they always show you a clip of the ending! The English language newspaper reviews have been remarking on this for years, but the TV companies don't seem to read these newspapers.

There are cable (BBC, CNN, Discovery and National Geographic Channels, etc.) and satellite (Star) systems available too, with sports channels on both.

Newspapers, magazines, libraries, books and CDs

Hong Kong has a very large publishing industry and the local Chinese are avid newspaper and magazine readers - from serious journals to gossip glossies. There are two English language newspapers, the *South China Morning Post* for good general news coverage (www.scmp.com)and *The Standard* which specializes in business news (www.thestandard.com.hk).

DO check the *Post* on Saturdays for jobs and on Sundays for a TV guide for the following week. Also for the *Trading Post*, which lists cheap second hand household goods, such as air-conditioners and freezers, for sale by people leaving Hong Kong. These are the famed (and stunningly unoriginal) lists which have dozens of ads starting 'Expat leaving...'. If you advertise here, **DO** try to make it more original, so you can get your ad noticed.

DO read Nury Vittachi's, Jason Wordie's and Kevin Sinclair's columns in the *South China Morning Post* and elsewhere. All are very knowledgeable about Hong Kong and its people and have a very affectionate take on our idiosyncrasies.

Public libraries in Hong kong are modern and highly computerized. **DO** have a look at the latest - the Hong Kong Central library in Causeway Bay. Its architecture is a cross between Chinese and Classical and is quite controversial. More convenient perhaps is the City Hall Library near the Star Ferry, Hong Kong side.

English language bookshops are found all over Hong Kong. **DO** try and get used to the prices. The mark-up for UK books is higher than US books. Local booksellers include Bookazine, Swindons, Page One and W.H. Smith (so far only at the airport, air-side).

For music CDs, VCDs and DVDs try HMV which has large stores both on Hong Kong Island and in Kowloon.

DO also shop in the smaller stores, because you can sometimes find bargains. Copyright piracy has been a blight on Hong Kong, but the police and customs services have been cracking down severely on pirates for a number of years.

But **DO** exercise some common sense...even if the CD looks OK, even if Whitney Houston's picture is on the front, if it's very cheap, it's probably:
a) a fake, or
b) a cover of the original music by an unknown Thai lady.

Museums

DO visit some of Hong Kong's many museums. Here are some highlights:

Museum of Teaware (Flagstaff House)
A whole museum to the glories of tea, located in Hong Kong's oldest colonial building (1846).

Hong Kong Racing Museum
At the Jockey Club, Happy Valley racecourse. A veritable shrine to the Hong Kong obsession for the horses.

Hong Kong Museum of Medical Sciences
In a lovely old building (1906) in the old Taipingshan area on Hong Kong Island. It has a replica of a Chinese medicine shop and some interesting exhibits and displays relating to Hong Kong's medical history.

Hong Kong Science and History Museums
Near the Cross-Harbour Tunnel Kowloon side, these two museums are great for kids.

Hong Kong Space Museum and Omnimax

Just opposite the Peninsula next to the Hong Kong Cultural Centre. Go to the show and then have high tea in the Peninsula afterwards!

Hong Kong Museum of Art

Also next to the Cultural Centre.

Hong Kong Museum of Coastal Defense

Built over fortifications at Lei Yue Mun.

Sheung Yiu Folk Museum

For the very adventurous - way out (three bus rides away from Star Ferry Kowloon) in Sai Kung country park in the New Territories. It's a fortified Hakka village built in the late nineteenth century.

Hong Kong Heritage Museum

A huge museum built in traditional Chinese style, located in Shatin in the New Territories.

Theme Parks

Ocean Park

This is a theme park with all the usual gut wrenching rides and a sea-world in a spectacular setting on a beautiful headland overlooking the South China Sea. It's worth going for the whole day, and there are family tickets. There's food in there, but **DO** take sun hats, because the place is quite exposed.

Once within the gates, Ocean Park has two centres, with a very long wonderful cable car ride in between the two (free once you're in, like everything else, except food and drink).

DO note that if you're meeting someone when leaving there are TWO exits, and they're at least 30 minutes walking/escalator ride (the longest in the world)/cable car distance from one another.

DO also note that the cable car closes before the Park does.

Disneyland

Due on Lantau Island in 2005. Watch this space.

ON THE TOWN:
NIGHTLIFE - ITS JOYS
AND TERRORS

HONG KONG

DON'T go believing Hong Kong is a second Bangkok. This is quite a straight town, but there's fun to be had from the innocent to the carnal, if that's what you want. It's a great town to have a night out in!

The **DO**s and **DON'T**s are fairly standard ones:

If you plan to taste the pleasures of the flesh, **DO** practice safe sex. If you can't avoid going for the full monty, always use a condom. Condoms can be bought from all pharmacies, supermarkets, and many of the smaller provision shops and of course the shops in your hotel. AIDS is in Hong Kong. Why take it home with you?

DO stay away from drugs, they're totally illegal here and not very good for your health!

DON'T drink yourself into oblivion: you could be robbed or tricked into parting with your credit card or expensive Swiss watch. And if you drink, **DON'T** drive.

DO plan your night out. Figure out your travel arrangements, how you'll get there, and how you'll get back (possibly the worse for wear). You'll look more like a local resident who knows what you're doing, and less like a tourist wandering aimlessly and ripe for plucking!

DO look confident and purposeful when you're on the streets (we know, it is difficult to look purposeful when you've had sixteen whiskeys....).

After a hard day's night on the town, **DON'T** fall asleep in a taxi or a bus. You'll get lost and you might end up having an altercation with a taxi driver about the fare. Either he'll drive you round forever to increase his income, or he'll be annoyed that he's got a drunken foreigner in his back seat he can't get rid of.

DO take with you the name card of where you're staying. The taxi driver can then read the address in Chinese characters on the card and know exactly where he's supposed to be going.

DO approach a policeman or policewoman for help if you get in any difficulties. Hong Kong has Asia's finest police force (TRUE!). Quite a few speak good English.

Advice for men

DON'T get friendly with our girls in the street, however pretty they are (and many of them are beautiful). Because Hong Kong is a relatively safe town, even in the red light districts, women passing you on the street may be wholly innocent ladies on their way home from work. If you touch them, you'll probably be arrested for assault.

DO be sure of your ground. Chinese women mostly find foreign men boorish and drink-laden. **DON'T** prove them right! Many women marry quite late here...they're choosy!

Unless you look like Brad Pitt of course, then you might stand a chance...

Advice for women

Single foreign women are mostly left alone in Hong Kong, although there have been cases of assault on crowded commuter trains.

If you go into a hotel bar alone in Hong Kong, you might be approached by a gigolo, looking for a free drink, or more, so **DO** beware!

DO walk in the opposite direction to traffic flow, in the MIDDLE of the pavement (sidewalk). If you do this:
• You won't be grabbed and pulled into a dark alley
• You won't have your bag snatched from behind by a motorcyclist or car driver
• You won't be bothered by curb crawlers

Money

DO hold on to your wallet!

DON'T leave your bag or haversack unattended. In bars, keep hold of it, or wrap it round a chair-leg.

DON'T go to the toilet and leave your bag behind.

DO watch out for pickpockets at all times.

Red lights

The main tourist red light districts are in Wanchai on the Island, and Tsim Sha Tsui in Kowloon. Locals mostly go to the area near Temple Street and Shanghai Street in Kowloon, off Nathan Road. We are told that the experience in all such places can be seedy and speedy.

Nightclubs and girlie bars

DO be very careful about these places!

DON'T be fooled! A sign saying 'NIGHTCLUB' in Hong Kong does not mean a disco. There are plenty of discos in Hong Kong which are advertised as such. A 'nightclub' is an ultra-expensive hostess bar.

Whether you want a hostess or not, she might sit down next to you and engage you in conversation. This can cost you a month's wages, because her drinks and her time are chargeable, sometimes at extortionate rates.

DON'T forget, as soon as you sit down, the clock is ticking and the dollars are mounting.

DON'T forget, in the girlie bars, you might go in on the promise of a cheap pint of beer, but the drinks for the girls dangling from your arms can cost hundreds of Hong Kong dollars each.

DON'T take your credit card into girlie bars. Use cash - at least there will be a limit to your spending! Some bars run off copies of credit cards. Others amend the total on their counterfoil. You will only discover the fraud days or weeks later.

If you do decide to charge it, **DON'T** give your credit card over to a nightclub hostess without checking on the scale of prices first, and in what currency services are offered. If they say 'dollars', check if it's HK or US.

Pubs and clubs

The main non-red light district is Lan Kwai Fong in Central, with a new extended arm up the Mid-Levels escalator to Soho. Lan Kwai Fong is full of bars and music...and theme restaurants. Soho is full of theme restaurants...and bars. Lan Kwai Fong can get very crowded on public holidays...especially during the December 31st new year celebrations. A tragic accident happened here a few years ago. People were trampled underfoot because there were just too many bodies in what is a very small area of steep streets.

Beer and spirits are expensive, though they are quite cheap in the supermarkets (the two main chains are Wellcome where they

sort of welcome you, and Park'N'Shop where you can't always park). Try the happy 'hour' in bars and hotels - some last as long as 6 to 7 hours. - when you get two drinks for the price of one.

There are bars in 5 star hotels and down back streets. There are topless bars, theme bars, English pubs, American bars, French bistros, Mexican cantinas, bars with live bands, or just bars with bars...you name it, it's in Hong Kong.

DO check if there are cover charges or entrance fees, and what the service charge might be.

You can usually eat in bars in Hong Kong.

DO read the daily newspapers, and the two freebies available in bars, bookshops, cafes, etc.: *bc Magazine* (monthly) and *HK Magazine* (weekly) for:
- Where to eat and drink;
- What's on;
- Who's in;
- Who's out:
- Where to listen to live music
- Where to get tickets.....etc.etc.

Karaoke

If this is your thing, these places are all over town. Young people (generally) hire a booth - with a CCTV camera installed to make sure they don't get too overt in their affection for their singing companion. You can get snacks and drinks in there. You select a track to sing to by using the computerised console. It's like a jukebox, except with Karaoke, you're in the Box.

Karaoke is also very popular for big events such as weddings and New Year dinners - along with *mahjong.*

RELIGION

All religions may be seen as having a basis in some kind of superstition. But they are also philosophies of life and the major Chinese 'religions' are no different in this regard.

DO note that we Chinese are perhaps more interested in aspects like fortune telling and auspicious events, signs, ceremonies and portents than Westerners, but it's only a matter of degree. Generally speaking, we are a very practical and pragmatic people.

In Hong Kong we worship our ancestors but may also revere the Buddha, the Dao (or Tao), Confucius, Jehovah, Mohammed, the Pope and the Protestant Reformation! Many of our visitors and temporary residents, such as the large population of Philippine maids, are also extremely devout. All told, we are great respecters of religions of all types.

DO not doubt that we are very tolerant in this regard.

Here's a brief introduction to the many somewhat confusing aspects of religion in Hong Kong.

Daoism, Buddhism, Confucianism and Ancestor Worship

There are more than 600 Chinese temples here. What are they all for and 'who' do we locals worship? When one enters a Chinese temple (and **DO** enter them, they are very informal places most of the time), one may recognise the statue of the Buddha, but...who are all those other deities and why are they sometimes in the same temple? Don't they get a temple or even a room of their own? Well, yes, they may be given that privilege, but we are happy to bundle them all together, along with reverence for our own ancestors and clan antecedents. We make sure we've covered all the possibilities and eventualities. So the Goddess of Mercy, Kuan Yin, is there for the rituals of daily life, as well as the Queen of Heaven, Tin Hau, to protect the fishermen, and of course the God of War, Kuan Ti, to instil righteousness!

We have gods for particular islands in Hong Kong, and gods for specific trades and daily actions. As you walk along the street, **DO** notice the small shrines on the pavements outside many doors, and shrines inside shops with fruit and red lights on them - for the door gods, the house gods, and the ancestors. If you look at the windows of a Hong Kong apartment block at night - particularly the darkened ones when the occupants are out on the town - notice the red glow from the lights of our family ancestral shrines.

Most of the deities are rooted in the Chinese Daoist (Taoist) religion. 'Dao' means 'the Way', and its tenets, first expounded by Laozi in the sixth century BC, are at once simple, yet ungraspable. As a 'way' of living and reducing the stress factors associated with modern life, Daoism has struck a chord with many Westerners who search for an uncomplicated ethos which emphasises quietude, compromise and achieving things by not over-achieving. Over two thousand years of Chinese history, this simple philosophy of life has developed another side - with vengeful gods who need to be assuaged - a Daoist pantheon which inhabits heavens and hells. The purists would call this side of Daoism, with its heavy emphasis on the supernatural, 'superstitious', but Chinese people have long considered it prudent and profitable to keep these gods happy when conducting their lives and their businesses. Daoism helps us achieve immortality. Hence the proliferation of deities and temples dedicated to each or all of the gods. Lighting a joss

stick to secure their patronage and achieve good fortune, or leaving offerings of fruit in their honour, or both, is merely the safe and sensible thing for us to do, particularly when planning for a long term afterlife.

Buddhist scriptures began to be imported into China around the first century AD. The religion is exemplified in Hong Kong by the largest outdoor bronze statue of the Buddha in the world, at the Po Lin Monastery on Lantau Island.

DO go and visit it, and have a vegetarian meal prepared by the monks who worship there.

Confucius lived in China from 551-479 BC. His philosophy of moral conduct in private and public life has had a profound influence on the history and politics of China. The rise and fall of the dynasties over the centuries, and the continued adherence to the Confucian written Classics of governance by one emperor after another, one dynasty after another, testify to the importance of his teachings.

Confucianism still finds a central place in the education of the young in Hong Kong. Many of our local schools are proud to state as their mission in their prospectuses that they instil the moral code of Confucius in their pupils. Local Confucians are now planning a temple to his name. Meanwhile, we follow the 'religion' or, more correctly, the moral code of Confucius, not by direct worship, but by bringing up our children according to his

precepts, impressing upon them their absolute lifelong duty to their family and their elders, and by conducting ourselves properly in our professional and business life. Lee Kwan Yew of Singapore has highlighted this code as a central buttress in the theory of a separate set of 'Asian values' which have allowed the Far East to develop so rapidly over the last 30 years.

Having said all that, we're not very outwardly formal in our religious practices in the Western sense. So, when you go to a Chinese temple, **DON'T** be surprised that:
- many of them are not very well looked after
- the interiors are dusty and full of smoke from joss sticks
- parts of them are devoted to ancestral tablets
- clothes may be hanging out to dry both inside and outside
- stray animals may be wandering around inside
- a TV may be on somewhere
- people may be sitting on the altar having a cigarette
- beggars could

be loitering outside (although the Hong Kong authorities do try to move them on)

And **DON'T** miss the following:

- **Man Mo Temple** in Hollywood Road on Hong Kong Island - for the forest of incense coils suspended from the ceiling
- The musty and atmospheric **Pak Tai Temple** on Cheung Chau Island for its historical relics
- **The Taoist Wong Tai Sin Temple** for its fortune tellers and joss stick-burning worshippers
- As noted above, **the giant Buddha** and **Po Lin Monastery** at Ngong Ping on Lantau Island for magnificent views and vegetarian food
- **The Che Kung Temple** in Shatin for the colourful paper windmills and gaudy talismans on sale nearby

Catholicism, Protestantism, Judaism, Islam, Hinduism, Sikhism and just about everything else...

Whatever your personal religious beliefs, Hong Kong will probably be able to accommodate you. The missionaries got here too so most of the denominations under the umbrella of the Protestant faith and Catholicism are present in the Hong Kong community. There are at least a quarter of a million Catholics in Hong Kong now.

Catholicism and Protestantism arrived with the first real invasion of Westerners into China after the first Opium War in the 1840s, and St. John's Cathedral in Central District dates from that time. Over the last 150 years or so, the various denominations have set up schools, colleges, hospitals and day-care centres, as well as cheaper well run guest houses like the Hong Kong YMCA and YWCA hotels. You don't have to be a Catholic or a Protestant to avail yourself of these benefits.

There are about 80,000 Muslims in Hong Kong. One of the most visible examples of their presence is the Kowloon Mosque on Nathan Road, where there has been a mosque since 1896.

DO visit the mosque outside prayer times, but ensure that your arms and legs are covered. Ladies should cover their heads with a scarf.

Three major synagogues cater for the spiritual needs of the 1,000-strong Jewish community.

The 12,000 Hindus conduct their religious observances at the Hindu Temple in Happy Valley.

Sikhs first came to Hong Kong as soldiers serving in the British armed forces, again in the late 1800s, and their temple is in Queen's Road East. Many Sikhs can still be seen guarding hotel entrances and generally building upon their deserved reputation for strength and reliability, developed over many years as soldiers and policemen.

Tourists from all around the world are welcome to visit church or temple when they come to Hong Kong. **DO** check the local press and attend a church service. Or **DO** go to a Chinese temple, light a joss stick and leave an offering. After all, freedom of religious belief is enshrined in Hong Kong's Basic Law.

As far as religion in Hong Kong is concerned, **DO** follow some general hints:

Photography

Some temples are historic sites and encourage tourism, so photography is OK there. Others may post signs prohibiting photography.

DO ask before taking pictures. We tend to be more sensitive in temples off the beaten track and for taking photos of ancestral tablets. If no-one is around, it should be fine, but **DO** be careful if people are worshipping or conducting ceremonies. It probably won't be welcome.

Services

There are usually services in temples only on specific festivals or special occasions, i.e., not regular services as in a church. Services at personal request are usually conducted at the requestor's venue, e.g., in our homes, or at a funeral. Catholic and Protestant Church services are listed in the English language newspaper, the *South China Morning Post*.

And here is some special information you probably won't find in other guidebooks:

What do we say when we're praying?

If we have special needs and go to the temple to ask the gods for help, we say a personal prayer. However, monks, nuns and dedicated Buddhists usually recite scriptures or prayers in their worship.

Can we ask about a person's religion?

We usually have a mixture of beliefs, so it might be considered a bit strange if you ask straight out "What religion are you?" It's not so cut and dried, but most people will probably be happy to expand a bit if you do ask the question. A foreigner was once asked by a colleague, "Are you a Catholic or a Christian?" - and since Catholics are also Christians, it may seem a surprising question. But then 'Christian' in Hong Kong usually means just 'Protestant' or perhaps 'Non-Conformist'.

Are there sects or cults in Hong Kong?

Yes, we've had our share of sects and cults but not on a wide scale and things seem to be a bit quiet at the moment. In 1996 there was a big outcry about the "Church of Zion" sect whose leader taught his 1,800 followers to drink hydrogen peroxide, for reasons best known to himself. Anyway the Government Social Welfare Department soon put a stop to it by threatening

to prosecute sect families which abused their children by feeding them the noxious chemical! Another cult in the 1980s tried to increase its (male) membership by urging female members to indulge in sexual seduction which was rather euphemistically called 'flirty fishing'.

In recent years there was a big *Falun Gong* convention in Hong Kong in support of fellow adherents on the Mainland. The authorities there (and also, it seems, even in post-handover Macao) have labelled the *Falun Gong* movement a 'counter-revolutionary cult', have banned it and imprisoned its followers. Its beliefs encompass ancient Chinese philosophies such as the spirit of *qi gong* which incorporates a system of breathing exercises for better health and deep meditation. *Qi* is a kind of life essence or life force running through each person; an individual, it is said, can lock into this and learn to control and exploit it. There is a magical, mystical element to *qi gong* as well which the Chinese Communist Party has always taken great exception to - *qi gong* practitioners were also vilified during the Cultural Revolution in the 1960s.

CHINESE FESTIVALS IN HONG KONG

Festivals are an integral part of our culture and daily lives and the dates on which they fall every year are determined by the lunar calendar. Without them, 90 percent of our public holidays would be no more!

- **Chinese New Year** is the Spring festival, the start of the lunar calendar. The date varies each year on the Western calendar, from late January to early February

- **Ching Ming** falls at the beginning of the third moon somewhere around the Easter period (March/April)

- **The Tin Hau Festival** falls on the twenty-third day of the third moon (April/May)

- **The Cheung Chau Bun Festival** falls on the eighth day of the fourth moon (April/May)

- **The Dragon Boat Festival** falls on the fifth day of the fifth moon (June)

- **The Yue Laan (Hungry Ghosts) Festival** falls on the fifteenth day of the seventh moon (Aug/Sept)

- **The Mid-Autumn Festival** falls on the fifteenth night of the eighth moon (Sept/Oct)

- **Chung Yeung** falls on the ninth day of the ninth moon (Sept/Oct)

- **The Winter Solstice Festival** falls on the eleventh moon (Dec)

Chinese New Year

This is our most important festival and the one time of the year when families must gather together to celebrate. Traditionally

Chinese New Year is celebrated over a period of 15 days, each of which involves its own special rituals and significance. The first three days are public holidays in Hong Kong.

DO remember that this is the one time in the year when almost every store will be closed and the hustle and bustle of this busy city will come to a halt. Business usually resumes on the fourth day but most Chinese stores will stay closed well past the seventh day.

In the weeks leading up to the festival, we buy new clothes, have a haircut, clean up our homes and give them a new coat of paint. There will also be beautiful flower markets held in various locations all over Hong Kong, the most popular taking place in Victoria Park on Hong Kong Island.

New Year's Eve

DO light up your home to get rid of evil spirits and to attract good fortune.

DO stay up to see in the New Year.

DO have a bath or shower on New Year's Eve in order to wash all the bad luck away.

DO pay off all your debts before New Year's Day.

DO hold a *tuen nin faan* (family reunion dinner) in order to keep the family clan together in the coming year.

DO put up *fai chun* - strips of red paper with auspicious

dos & don'ts **in HONG KONG**   143

Chinese sayings on them - on each side of your front door.

DO go to the flower market to buy some peach blossom, chrysanthemums and other flowers, or an orange tree. And if you want to save money, **DO** go there after midnight to pick up some bargains when prices plunge as the New Year dawns.

New Year's Day

DO put on new clothes and shoes to visit relatives and friends.

DO greet people you meet with *'Gung Hei Faat Choi'*, meaning 'Wishing you great prosperity', which is the traditional 'hello' at this time.

DO give *laisee* - red packets containing money for luck - to children and the unmarried.

DON'T sweep the floor or you'll sweep your wealth away.

DON'T wash your hair or you'll wash your wealth away as well.

DO stick to vegetarian food and **DON'T** eat meat as it's bad luck to slaughter poultry on New Year's Day.

Second Day

DO present offerings such as joss sticks, roast pig and fruit to your ancestors as today you are allowed to slaughter livestock.

DO find a good spot to watch the firework display in the harbour. A hotel room or restaurant overlooking the harbour would be ideal.

Third Day

DO stay at home to avoid disagreements and arguments among friends and family.

Seventh Day

This is *Yan Yat* (Everyone's birthday) so **DO** get together for a celebration and to eat the traditional rice porridge.

Fifteenth Day

This day is known as the Spring Lantern Festival and also as Chinese Valentine's Day when lovers meet to celebrate. This is the last day of the New Year celebrations and the final opportunity to give or receive *laisee*. **DO** take a look at all the lovely lanterns which will be on display throughout the city.

At Chinese New Year

DON'T let off firecrackers although they're supposed to exorcise evil spirits. Firecrackers are still widely used in the celebration of Chinese festivals in the Mainland and Macau, but are banned in Hong Kong and increasingly restricted in Mainland cities.

DO place Door-Gods by your front door to protect the household from evil spirits.

DO provide traditional snacks for friends and relatives. The names of foods eaten at this special time usually have special meanings, e.g., *lin ji* (lotus seeds) which also means 'one son after another' or *nin go* (New Year cake) which is cake made from glutinous rice. The word 'go' means 'cake' but sounds like the word for 'tall' which indicates a person will grow in status, riches, etc. during the coming year.

DO give *laisee* to newspaper boys, delivery people, dry cleaners and building caretakers but **DON'T** give any to public servants (e.g., the postman or dustman) or people working in quasi-governmental organisations as it is against the law, supposedly to prevent corruption.

DO walk around the peach blossom tree for luck if you're still single without a date. This will ensure the love angel will look kindly on you.

DON'T pick the flowers from peach blossom trees or the fruits from kumquat trees.

DON'T bargain on the third day of the Lunar New Year - the first day the wet market re-opens - hawkers won't treat you kindly if you do.

Ching Ming Festival

During Ching Ming, the entire family pays their respects to our ancestors buried in the hills and cemeteries. It's also a day for the family to welcome the arrival of Spring.

DO visit ancestral graves and take with you incense (believed to be food for the spirit), fruit and other offerings. These may include money (sheets of white paper cut to the size of real currency), models of cars, houses, gold bars, etc., to be burnt before the grave for the use and enjoyment of the deceased.

DO pay your respects by holding three incense sticks before you and bowing three times in front of the tombstone. The incense sticks must be offered in multiple of threes. Some of us may also place three Chinese wine glasses there and offer a drink to our ancestors by pouring the wine from left to right in front of the tombstone.

DO leave a pile of fake paper money on top of the tombstone. This signifies that the deceased is remembered and visited by his/her descendants.

It's customary to consume the food offerings to bring peace to the family so **DO** find a suitable place nearby and enjoy a picnic with the family.

DO go kite flying. This is a traditional Ching Ming activity

practised for centuries. In the Ching Dynasty, wooden pipes were attached to the kite so that when the wind blew, it would produce music. The louder the music, the better the luck the family would have during the year. Nowadays, kite flying competitions are still very popular at the Ching Ming Festival.

DON'T step over any tombstones in the cemeteries as it's a sign of disrespect to the deceased.

DON'T pick up any paper money, coins or offerings intended to be burnt for ancestors. Those are considered to belong to the deceased who may request you to return them.

DON'T return home immediately after visiting the cemetery as it may bring bad luck to the household.

So **DO** go to a restaurant or café and leave your bad luck behind before returning home.

Tin Hau Festival

The Tin Hau Festival celebrates the birthday of the most popular patron of boat people - Tin Hau, the Goddess of the Sea. On this day, all kinds of small boats are decorated with multicoloured pennants and loaded with offerings to the goddess as people make their way to one of the many Tin Hau temples to pray for plentiful catches, good weather and safe voyages.

DO join the thousands of boat people, residents and other tourists who go to Joss House Bay where a large temple is dedicated to Tin Hau and **DO** enjoy the lion dances and parades which are held there.

Cheung Chau Bun Festival

The Cheung Chau Bun Festival is a week long holiday on the island of Cheung Chau where offerings are made to placate the spirits of the dead, possibly those killed by pirates for which the island was once notorious. The highlight of the festival is on the evening of the third night, after the spirits have had their feast, when the villagers used to climb special towers made of buns. This practice of scrambling for buns which are meant to bring good luck was discontinued some years ago after one of the towers collapsed and injured some of the crowd.

DO visit Cheung Chau during the Bun Festival to enjoy the parades, colourful floats, Chinese operas and bun towers but **DON'T** climb the towers unless you want to end up in hospital.

Dragon Boat Festival

The Dragon Boat Festival commemorates the death long ago of Qu Yuan, a poet and great patriot who lived at a time when China was divided into many small states, each ruled by an emperor. Wrongly accused of betraying the emperor, he threw himself into a river and drowned. To commemorate his death,

dragon
boat races
are held in the
hope that the loud
noise from the drums and
cheers from the onlookers will
scare away the fish that will otherwise consume Qu Yuan's corpse.

DO go to the boat races to see the magnificent brightly painted boats and **DO** cheer them on to help scare away the fish. If you know the right people you might be able to join a team yourself but - Public Health Warning: **DO** make sure you're fit and **DO** avoid taking a mouthful of harbour water. One oarsman had an experience with a dead fish which had elastoplast wrapped around it!

DO eat the dumplings which are specially made at this time. Legend has it that when Qu Yuan died, people threw glutinous rice dumplings into the river hoping that the fish would feed on them instead of on his corpse.

DO give dumplings as presents for family and friends but **DON'T** throw dumplings into Hong Kong waters unless you want to be fined for littering.

Yue Laan (Hungry Ghosts) Festival

This festival commemorates the period when the spirits of the dead roam the world. During the Feast, people offer prayers and food to all the spirits in general, and especially to the departed who have no relatives/families to do so for them. Paper money is burnt by the roadside and food, fruit and wine are offered to appease the ghosts.

DO burn joss sticks and offer your ancestors things for their daily needs, e.g. paper money, cars, houses, clothes, *mahjong* sets, TVs, etc.

DON'T stay out late at night unless you want to bump into the spirits and **DON'T** pick up any paper money or food from the street because the ghosts will demand their return.

Mid-Autumn Festival

The seventh, eighth and ninth months are the three autumn months in the Chinese calendar. The Mid-Autumn Festival takes place on the fifteenth day of the eighth month when there's a full moon. Traditionally it's a festival which is a family celebration.

In Hong Kong, we all go out into the streets and parks to gaze at the beautiful full moon and enjoy ourselves with our children who carry illuminated lanterns of all different colours, shapes and sizes. We also eat mooncakes which are very rich and filling.

DO celebrate with the whole family as the full moon signifies a happy conclusion to everything.

And **DO** lay out offerings of fruit, nuts, taro and mooncakes in the garden or on the window-sill so the Moon God can see them.

DO share the offerings, especially the mooncakes which are said to bring good luck. They should be divided equally amongst everyone present (pregnant women should get two or more shares!). But **DON'T** try to eat too much as they are very heavy on the stomach.

DO go to Victoria Park on Hong Kong Island which will be packed with families and lanterns, and **DO** take time to admire the full moon.

And **DON'T** forget your camera or you'll regret it! This is a really colourful and enjoyable festival.

Chung Yeung Festival

This is also a major celebration for commemorating the dead. On this day, we make our way to high ground to ward off future disasters. Ancestral graves are also visited, swept and honoured.

As on Ching Ming, **DO** stay away from the New Territories as thousands travel out there to visit the graves and cemeteries at this time.

Winter Solstice Festival

The Winter Solstice Festival falls on the longest night of the year, December 21, which is also the shortest day of the year. All businesses, factories, offices and schools close early for families to spend the evening together. We consider this festival to be almost as important as Chinese New Year as it signifies that all the work in the fields has been completed for the year and all the

crops are safely stacked away, allowing the farmers time to prepare for the Lunar New Year celebration. **DO** remember that restaurants and stores close early on this day for family celebrations.

Miscellaneous festivals

As for other festivals, and there are many others, consider the following:

A recent photo in the *South China Morning Post* was captioned:
  'Devil of a job. Two women use their shoes to 'beat up devil men' in a rite in Tai Kok Tsui yesterday. The rite is part of the Feast of Excited Insects, or Chingche, meaning 'arousing from hibernation'. People use the day to put curses on their enemies by paying others to beat paper effigies'.

BIRTHS AND BIRTHDAYS

Chinese really love children and not so long ago we all liked to have large families. Traditionally, we've always been keen to have boys because they carry on the family line and are supposed to look after their parents in their old age and honour them and their ancestors once they have passed away. We used to try and try for a boy, even if it meant having 11 or 12 girls first (yes - one of the authors really knows a family with this unfortunate experience). But nowadays, things are different. Bringing up a family in Hong Kong is expensive. Many wives go out to work and we prefer to spend our hard earned money on our homes, on leisure activities, eating out and travel. So now we just have small families and some of us are quite happy to have even just one girl or one boy.

Usually we try to have a child pretty soon after getting married, not only for the joy a child brings, but also because it's still very important for parents to have someone to look after them in their old age and to honour them and their ancestors once they've passed on. When the child is born, it's usually given a name, the first part of which is the family generation name. So **DON'T** be surprised to find that siblings have similar-sounding names.

Children's names were traditionally chosen by the paternal grandparents but nowadays the parents will probably choose the name themselves. Many of us like to give our children Western names as well so, as we said before, **DO** expect we Hong Kong Chinese to have quite a complicated set of names.

After the baby arrives, it used to be the tradition for the mother to rest at home with it for one month or more. She wasn't allowed to have a bath or wash her hair during this period of time. Nowadays this isn't so common. But most mothers are still given a nutritious brew of ginger, pig's trotters and boiled eggs in a heavily sweetened vinegar soup to eat. This is called *geung cho*.

DON'T be taken aback if you're offered some when you visit and **DO** try a spoonful. It's actually quite delicious, though very rich.

After one month, we hold a dinner for relatives and close friends to celebrate the new baby's arrival. This is called the baby's *moon yuet* and is traditionally the first time it's taken out of the home. On this occasion, friends and relatives bring expensive presents for the baby, such as a gold chain, a jade bracelet, or lucky sums of money in red *laisee* packets. A lucky red packet containing a small amount of money will be handed to them in return to thank them. The family may also give visitors boiled eggs dyed an auspicious red.

DO take them with you when you leave. They're perfectly edible.

We don't celebrate birthdays as much as Westerners do but we do have big bashes for our menfolk when they reach 60 and on each successive decade. For women, it's 61 and each successive decade. Usually we celebrate by having a special meal for friends and family. The wealthier we are, the more extravagant will be the meal, and the more people invited, including business associates and office colleagues. Traditional presents include *gam paai* (gold ingots) or *laisee* (lucky money) to buy something that they want. If you get invited, **DO** go along and join in the celebrations.

MARRIAGES

When we get married in Hong Kong we often follow a mix of Western and Chinese practices. Our families first decide on an auspicious day for the marriage. We then hold a ceremony in a church or registry office by a Chinese banquet for family, relatives and friends later that day or some days afterwards. Normally the groom's family foots the bill, but this is changing and increasingly both parties tend to share the expense.

The most important event is the wedding banquet which is usually held in a Chinese restaurant. Once that's over, it means we're truly married. Even if we don't get married in a church, the bride often dresses up in a white western bridal gown to have photographs taken, then switches to a red Chinese wedding dress for the Chinese banquet. To announce the wedding, the family will send out red cake coupons which you can exchange for cakes from whichever chain of bakeries provides the coupons.

Banquets are expensive and often put a young couple in debt for a considerable time. Guests sit at round tables with usually 12 people per table. The extravagance of the banquet is appreciated by the number of tables there are, and the more guests we invite, the more likely it is we'll recoup most of the money we've spent as people almost always give money as a gift.

At the banquet, as the guests file in:

DO sign your name on the piece of red silk which is a souvenir for the couple.

DO give a present of a *lai guen* (gift certificate) or *laisee* (red packet of lucky money). The gift certificate can be bought from any bank and red *laisee* packets can be bought from stationery shops and street hawkers. The money helps pay for the banquet and there will be a current rate expected, depending on the closeness of your relationship to the married couple. A lucky red packet with a small coin in it will be handed back to you in thanks.

Before the banquet begins, the tables, which are basically small and round, will probably be used for *mahjong* sessions for several hours. When it's time to eat, the waiters bring in large round table tops, already laid, and place them on top of the small tables. At this stage photographs are taken of all the guests with the bride and bridegroom.

DO take a look at the bride's beautifully embroidered *kei po* (Chinese wedding dress).

DON'T be envious that she wears a lot of bright yellow 24K gold jewellery. These will be gifts from family and relatives and are a sign of good fortune and prosperity.

The banquet usually consists of ten courses beginning with cold cuts, such as suckling pig, and ending with noodles, rice, small cakes and fruit.

DON'T eat too much of each course or you'll find it difficult to last to the end. The waiters and other guests will put more onto your plate if you eat everything up, so

DON'T be afraid to leave some bits and pieces to indicate you've had enough of that course. The dirty plates and bowls are usually replaced with clean ones when certain courses are finished so

DON'T be alarmed if your food is suddenly whisked away from you.

During the meal, the bride and bridegroom and their immediate family members move from table to table toasting the guests.

DO stand up and drink a toast with them.

At the end of the banquet, as soon as the fruit appears, the guests will probably take it, get up, and leave with amazing rapidity.

DO leave straightaway and take the fruit with you too. The families of the bride and bridegroom will line up by the door and shake the hands of the guests as they leave and thank them for attending the banquet.

DO join the queue to congratulate the families and wish the couple every happiness.

DEATHS

You can expect to come across both church and Chinese traditional funeral ceremonies in Hong Kong and Christian ceremonies may well include many elements of traditional Chinese funeral rites. Because land is expensive, dying is also very costly. We save up for years to have sufficient funds for our own coffin and funeral service. Poorer families often pay for the simplest rites which will take place perhaps at a Buddhist temple. Here the deceased will be laid behind a screen or curtain while the family, dressed in white, will be seated on the floor in front, receiving visitors and mourning the dead through the night over several days.

DON'T be surprised to find Buddhist priests sitting opposite the mourners and rather dispassionately folding small pieces of paper and intoning prayers without any expression.

Others may hire a small or large hall in a funeral parlour, depending on how much they can afford. Our funeral parlours are multi-storey buildings with each floor divided into halls of various sizes where services are conducted. The largest funeral parlours are located in North Point on Hong Kong Island and Hung Hom in Kowloon. For the convenience of mourners, wreaths can be purchased right outside the funeral parlour and delivered immediately to the relevant hall. A large photograph of the deceased will be displayed at the far end of the hall facing the entrance. Wreaths of flowers, usually on wooden frames, will be stacked all around the room and the photograph.

Although many customs are now 'dying' out (forgive the pun), mourners may wear black armbands and sober clothing for a certain number of months/weeks afterwards, and (depending on their relationship to the deceased), women may wear a small white (father), blue (mother) or green (grandparents) woollen flower in their hair. A small ancestral altar will be kept in many of our homes to allow us to continuously pay respect to deceased family members.

Before the funeral, families will prepare paper models of items which the deceased used in their lifetime, for example, cars, houses, portable phones, TV sets, etc., for use in the after-life. These can be quite spectacular, fascinating, gaudy and colourful works of art (see the section on Shopping: Paper Shops for further details). Before sunset on the eve of the funeral, the items will be burnt at the roadside or in a special room in the funeral parlour.

Usually the deceased is placed in an open casket behind the altar, but sometimes the casket will be brought out in the centre of the room. When the memorial service begins, mourners will be invited to file round the casket to take a last look at the deceased. A group of musicians may play funeral dirges on Chinese trumpets during the ceremony.

When you arrive at the funeral home, you'll be received by a relative of the dead, accompanied to the photograph at the altar, and expected to bow your head three times as the *tong gwoon* (funeral parlour official) calls out instructions. Some of the mourners may also place three incense sticks in an urn on an altar below the photograph.

DO turn to the bereaved family members standing on the left, and bow three times to them. They will then bow to you in return. You may be asked if you would like to see the deceased and, if you're up for it, it is polite and sensitive to agree. You will be taken to gaze upon the deceased for a few moments then led back to a seat to sit in contemplation or talk quietly to other mourners whilst various funeral rites take place. A Taoist funeral service is very colourful and full of activity. The priests wear beautiful robes and various ceremonies are carried out to lead the spirit of the deceased into the next world.

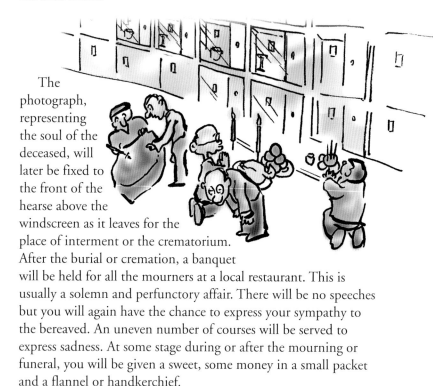

The photograph, representing the soul of the deceased, will later be fixed to the front of the hearse above the windscreen as it leaves for the place of interment or the crematorium. After the burial or cremation, a banquet will be held for all the mourners at a local restaurant. This is usually a solemn and perfunctory affair. There will be no speeches but you will again have the chance to express your sympathy to the bereaved. An uneven number of courses will be served to express sadness. At some stage during or after the mourning or funeral, you will be given a sweet, some money in a small packet and a flannel or handkerchief.

The period of interment in urban Hong Kong is very short as burial space can only be rented due to the high price and shortage of land. The deceased's remains will have to be dug up after 5 years or so and transferred to urns placed in a columbarium which may be located in the same cemetery. On hillsides in the New Territories, you'll come across burial urns containing remains of the dead, and traditional Chinese horseshoe graves where whole families may be interred together. Both urns and traditional graves will be located where the *fung shui* is favourable.

DO send a wreath to express your sympathy with the relatives of the deceased. These can be purchased at any flower shop, or outside a funeral parlour, and will be sent to the correct place at the correct time on your behalf.

DO make sure it's composed of flowers of an appropriate type and colour - the shopkeeper will be happy to advise. Flowers associated with death are lilies and frangipani.

DO express your sympathy personally to the family of the deceased.

DO make sure that what you wear is modest and an appropriate sober colour. Those associated with death are white and pale colours. Black is also acceptable.

DON'T feel obliged to wear hats, veils or gloves. It isn't necessary in Hong Kong.

DON'T sit at the front of the hall because it's reserved for close relatives.

DON'T take photos at the funeral parlour.

DON'T take photos of funeral processions or burning rituals.

DO follow the instructions of the priest or official at the funeral parlour during the ceremony.

DO give a monetary token to the bereaved, but make sure it's an odd sum to indicate sorrow (e.g., $101).

DO eat the sweet that will be given to you by the family of the deceased to take away the bitter taste of death.

DO spend the funeral money before you arrive home to get rid of the bad luck.

DO wash your hands and dry them on the flannel provided to wash away the bad luck but **DON'T** take the flannel home with you.

DO stay for at least half an hour or longer at the wake to show your respect for the dead and **DO** time your departure so that it doesn't disrupt any ceremonies.

DO leave the funeral parlour when the casket is about to be closed but **DON'T** arrive after the casket is closed or it will mean bad luck for the living.

DO bow your head to the family and relatives of the deceased as you leave and **DON'T** go straight home after the funeral or you'll take the bad luck home.

DO visit the cemeteries in Hong Kong. Located on steep hillsides with good *fung shui*, gravestones crowded together bearing photographs of the deceased, they're a really incredible sight.

GENERAL
INFORMATION

Useful telephone numbers and web sites

(**DO** *remember that, apart from* **999**, *phone numbers frequently change in Hong Kong*)

Emergency Services (Police, Fire, Ambulance)	**999**

In an emergency, call the hotel doctor, or **999**, *or the following casualty (ER) hospitals:*

• **Queen Mary Hospital**	**2855 4111**
Pokfulam, HK Island	
• **Queen Elizabeth Hospital**	**2958 8888**
Gascoigne Road, Kowloon	
• **Prince of Wales Hospital**	**2632 2211**
Shatin, New Territories	

Hong Kong medical services are very good, but can be very expensive for non-residents, so **DO** *make sure you're insured!*

HONG KONG GOVERNMENT   www.info.gov.hk/eindex.htm
HONG KONG TOURISM BOARD   www.discoverhongkong.com

Multilingual hotline	**2508 1234**

Shopfronts:
* Hong Kong International Airport Buffer Halls and transfer Area E2
* Star Ferry Concourse, Tsim Sha Tsui, Kowloon
* Ground Floor, The Centre, 99, Queen's Road Central

TELEPHONE SERVICES

Operator assisted service	**10010**
International service enquiry	**10013**
Directory enquiries	

- English **1081**   - Cantonese **1083**   - Putonghua **1088**

OTHER

Consumer Council	**2929 2222**
Community Advice Bureau	**2815 5444**
Immigration hotline	**2824 6111**
Road Co-op Lost and Found 24-hour free hotline	
for property lost in taxis	**1872 920**

Climate

January to March   cold
   DO get a reverse cycle air-conditioner.
April to June   rainy
   DO buy an umbrella
July to September   hot and sticky, blowy AND rainy
   DO stay indoors during a typhoon and 'black' rainstorm (*).
The humidity causes non-locals to wear three shirts a day
(minimum).
October to December   very nice, thank you! Cool, dry, blue skies.
   DO time your visit for these months if you can.

   (*) Typhoon warnings usually start with a signal No.3 being
hoisted by the Observatory. This information will be displayed in
the corner of your TV screen, or broadcast on the radio. Why '3'?
Who knows? Anyway, **DO** take notice, because it means there's a
typhoon coming, so get ready just in case. The signal then jumps
to '8' for some reason, everything shuts down and everyone, we
mean everyone, goes home and stays indoors.

   DO stay indoors during a Typhoon 8 (or over). They can be
VERY dangerous. Big heavy air-conditioners have been known to
be blown across the room from the galeforce winds outside. So
DO get your plants in from the balcony.

   Rainstorm warnings are the same. 'RED' means be very
careful, and 'BLACK' means go for shelter and don't move.

   DO heed the rainstorm warnings. Water can sheet down from
the skies in absolute torrents, filling up dry riverbeds and nullahs
to the brim, and, worst of all, undermining hillsides which slip
and bury everything in their path.

   You won't believe the force of these weather patterns until you
experience it for yourself. Deaths resulting from them are
thankfully uncommon, but they do happen, so **DO** be careful.

Useful words and phrases

The romanization of Cantonese words and phrases throughout the book generally follows the Sidney Lau system used in his *A Practical Cantonese-English Dictionary*, Hong Kong, Government Printer, 1977.

1. Words peculiar to our city which you may have never heard or seen before and may never hear or see again:

Amah   Female Chinese servant (Transliteration of Cantonese: *a ma* - grandmother/father's mother).

Chop   Stamp or seal (**DO** beware: to 'chop' something in Hong Kong means to stamp it with a stamp or seal, not to 'hack' at it).

Comprador   Chinese merchant who acts as middleman in negotiations and trade between Chinese and foreigners. Not mentioned any longer except in history books and Clavell novels. (Portuguese: *comparator* - buyer).

Fung shui   Geomancy, literally 'wind water'. Spelling generally used in English. Correct romanization in Cantonese should be *fung sui*.

Godown   Warehouse. (Malay: *gudang* - warehouse).

Hong   Large trading house with a *taipan* (see below) in charge

Joss   Word used by foreign writers and other strange people to mean 'luck' as in 'good joss', 'bad joss'. Absolutely not used anywhere or by any self-respecting person in Hong Kong. (Portuguese: *deos* - god).

Junk   Traditional Chinese boat in all the paintings, with or without spectacular sail, with or without powerful engine. (Javanese: *jong* - flat-bottomed boat).

Laisee   Lucky money in special red packet.

Nullah	Nasty deep channel for waste water which people often fall into. (Hindi: *nala* - brook/ravine)).
Rickshaw	Small red shaded vehicle pulled by very old men located at Star Ferry on Hong Kong Island. The only form of transport in the olden days but now a tourist attraction. Short for Cantonese *yan lik che* (man power vehicle).
Sampan	Small boat usually propelled by woman with a pole. Transliteration of Cantonese *saam baan* (three planks).
Shroff	Place where you pay when you park in a car park. (Hindi/Arabic: *sarraf* - money-changer).
Taipan	Foreign merchant, head of large trading house (*hong),* wealthy and powerful enough to call the shots in governing the colony. Transliteration of Cantonese *daai baan* (big boss). Now only used in history books and Clavell novels.
Typhoon	Powerful, destructive wind, an oriental hurricane which brings Hong Kong to a standstill. Transliteration of Cantonese *daai fung* (big wind).

2. Words you may be able to use if you pluck up courage (using Sidney Lau's romanization system):

Greetings

Ha lo	Hello (to foreigner)
Jo san	Good morning
Jo tau	Goodnight
Joi gin	Goodbye
Baai baai	Bye bye
Gung hei faat choi	Chinese New Year greeting ('Congratulations and may you become prosperous')

General

Ai ya!	(used as a first reaction whenever anything goes wrong)

M goi	Thank you (for a service or kind act)
Doh je	Thank you (for a present)
Ma ma dei	So so
Dak haan	Free, nothing to do
Mo man tai	OK, no problem
Dak	OK (can be done)
M dak	Not possible, can't be done
Dim gaai	Why?
Dui m jue	Sorry, excuse me
Faat daat	Get rich (what everyone in Hong Kong is trying to do)
Fong bin	Convenient
M fong bin	Not convenient
Ho	Very (e.g. ho gwooi = very tired)
Ho ho	OK, nice
M ho	Don't! Stop it! Not nice, no good
M hai	No, is not
Yau chin	Rich
Mo chin	Poor
Leng	Pretty, lovely
M leng	Not very pretty
Mo lai maau	Rude, impolite
Chi sin	Crazy, nuts (what bus drivers say when they don't like what you've done)
Gong tong wa	Speak Cantonese language
Sik gong	I can speak the language
M sik gong	I can't speak the language, I don't know how to say it
Sik yin	To smoke
M ho sik yin	Don't smoke
Mo min	Lose 'face'
Gau chat	(19)97
Wooi gwai	Hong Kong's return to China in 1997
Chin	Money (what makes Hong Kong tick)
Laap saap	Rubbish (something discarded)
Faai wa	Rubbish (spoken)
Mo lei tau	Nonsense (nouveau slang)

Sau tai din wa	Portable phone
Gaat jaat	Cockroach (you're bound to see at least one in Hong Kong)
Ngaan geng	Specs, glasses
Ngan hong	Bank
Din no	Computer
Din si	TV
Din wa	Telephone
Din ying	Film, movie
San fan jing	ID card
Woo jiu	Passport

People

Gwai lo	Foreign person
Gwai poh	Foreign woman
Sai yan	Caucasian foreigner (literally 'Western person')
Gung yan	Household help

Forms of address

A sam	Auntie (polite address for middle-aged woman)
A poh	Grandma (polite address for elderly woman)
A suk	Uncle (polite address for middle-aged man)
A baak	Grandpa (polite address for elderly man)
Sin saang	Sir, Mr
Taai taai	Madam, Mrs
Siu je	Miss (young lady)
Mooi mooi	Little girl
Sai lo	Little boy
Siu pang yau	Little boy/girl (literally 'little friend')
Bi bi	Baby

Eating

Sik faan	To eat
Yam cha	Same as *'dim sam'*
Dim sam	Cantonese lunch, *'dim sum'*
Daan taat	Egg tart (very delicious)

Faai ji	Chopsticks
Laat	Spicy
Maai daan	May I have the bill?
Chaan teng	Restaurant
Cha lau	Restaurant
Hui yam cha	Go to have *dim sam*
Hui sik faan	Go to eat

Shopping

Maai ye	To shop, buy something
Paai dui	Queue up
Taai doh chin	Too expensive (literally: too much money)
Taai gwai	Too expensive
Taai daai	Too big
Taai sai	Too small
Ho peng	Very cheap
Gong ga	To bargain
Cheung saam	*Cheongsam*, figure-hugging Chinese traditional dress
Maai saam	Buy clothes
Gaau doi	Plastic bag (Hong Kong is full of them)
Hui maai ye	Go shopping
Yiu paai dui	You must queue up
Gong m gong ga?	Can we bargain?

Weather

Tin hei	Weather
Tin hei ho	The weather is good
Tin hei m ho	The weather isn't good
Lok yu	It's raining
Ho laang	Very cold
Ho yit	Very hot
Yi ga lok yue	It's raining now
Gam yat tin hei ho	Today's a nice day

Transport

Ba si	Bus

Siu ba	Minibus
Dik si	Taxi
Din che	Tram
Dei ha tit	MTR, subway, underground
KCR	KCR train
Tin Sing Ma Tau	Star Ferry
Gei cheung	Airport
Daap che	Go by bus (or other vehicle)
M goi yau lok	Please let me get off here (say this loudly when you want the minibus driver to stop)

Health

Yi yuen	Hospital
Yi saang	Doctor
Sue fuk	Well
M sue fuk	Not well
Yau beng	Ill
Tau tung	Headache
Tou tung	Stomach ache
Tau wan	Dizzy, faint
Tung	Hurts, painful
Ho tung	It's very painful
M tung	It doesn't hurt
Hui taai yi saang	Go to the doctor

Recreation

Da ma jeuk	Play *mahjong*
Paau ma	Horse racing
Pa saan	Hiking
Paau bo	Go jogging
Yau sui	Swimming
Da boh	Play a ball game